Mohonk: Its People and Spirit
A History of One Hundred Years of Growth and Service

by Larry E. Burgess, Archivist
A.K. Smiley Public Library, Redlands, California

Nineteen Hundred Eighty
Corrected and Updated 1993.

Published by
Purple Mountain Press, Ltd.
Main Street, P.O. Box E3
Fleischmanns, New York 12430
914-254-4062

ISBN 0-935796-42-8

Quotation on page 87: © 1971 by The New York Times Company. Reprinted by permission.
Quotation on page 47 with permission of Laurence M. Hauptman and Clearwater Publishing Co.

Library of Congress Cataloging in Publication Data:

Burgess, Larry E   1945 -
        Mohonk, its people and spirit.

        Includes index.
        1. Mohonk Mountain House - History.   2. Smiley family.
I. Title.
TX941.M63B87   647'.94747'3401   80-15087

Contents

Introduction

In the year 1911 Frederick E. Partington, then a devoted and perceptive member of the Mohonk House staff, penned a delightful book which he called "The Story of Mohonk". At that time Mohonk under ownership of the Smiley family was just over forty years old. The enterprise was surely so fresh and so rapidly expanding until that time that no one had thought of writing its history.

The Partington story forms the basis for three later editions of "The Story of Mohonk". In the second edition (published in 1932) an account of the twenty-year period, 1911 to 1930, was added, along with new illustrations. The third edition, published in 1950, did not enlarge the historical text, but added a chronology and a list of flora and fauna. And finally, the fourth edition added a third piece of writing, bringing the account up to 1960, so that the book covered 90 years of operation. Another significant addition to this edition was a brief preamble called "The Earlier History of the Shawangunks Around Mohonk". These two supplements were written by A. Keith Smiley, with full recognition that a person living so close to the scene of action and at a time so soon after events took place, lacked the capability of making objective judgments as to the historical importance of certain happenings.

Now that Mohonk's resort history covers well over a hundred years, it is agreed by the members of the Mohonk family that it is time for both an updating and a new perspective. We are indeed fortunate in having a good friend available to write a new history of Mohonk. Larry E. Burgess, who is a Redlands, California, resident, the winter home of Albert the twin and his brother Daniel, has the rare combination of keen interest in history, thorough knowledge of Mohonk and its people, and the necessary perspective.

The editor of this volume speaks for the author and the members of the Smiley family in the following message to readers. It does not seem possible to improve on the way in which it was expressed by Frederick Partington, in the second sentence of his preface:

"We sincerely trust that the book will fully gratify those who have expressed their desire for such a work, and wish to assure them that it is in every respect a token of good will and affection to all who care for, or are interested in, the story of Mohonk."

A. Keith Smiley
Mohonk Lake
New Paltz, New York
March 1990

Preface

When approached by members of the Smiley family about writing a new version of the history of their resort, Mohonk Mountain House, I was delighted and also apprehensive. In 1969 I had studied the lives of Mohonk's founder, Albert K. Smiley, his twin brother, Alfred, and their half-brother, Daniel. That initial project produced a privately printed volume and led me to pursue the study of the Lake Mohonk Conferences on the Indians for my doctoral dissertation. Fate or irony or luck then led me to the position of Archivist and Head of Special Collections at the A.K. Smiley Public Library in Redlands, California.

Though I believed that I knew Mohonk well, I was apprehensive about integrating the history of this remarkable enterprise so as to satisfy long-time guests and supporters, people who had not previously heard about the resort, and especially members of the Smiley family, a number of whom have been inextricably bound up in Mohonk's operation for many years.

As indicated in the Introduction, earlier Mohonk histories have all been titled "The Story of Mohonk" and have undergone several enlargements in the form of new editions. My effort, agreed upon by mutual decision with members of the Smiley family, is a completely new story about Mohonk. There is much yet to be written, and as is usual, much that had to be left out. Certain parts of Frederick E. Partington's original account are quoted at length in this volume so as to preserve some of the original flavor.

Many people were helpful in the production of this volume. Among these were: Jane Smiley who supplied material from Mohonk records and examined text for accuracy and style; Rachel O. Smiley, who kindly and stoically assisted in efforts to bridge the generations; Ruth Smiley, who supplied photographs and suggested additions of other material; Ben and Rachel Matteson, whose editorial comments broadened the scope of subjects; Daniel Smiley, who provided invaluable resources; Carolyn Fiske, Mohonk's Program Director, who reviewed the text and managed production and printing procedures; Monty Montaño, who prepared the index; Frank Wright, of Hefferan, Hastie & Leibman, Inc. whose concern and assistance went far beyond the usual functions of layout and design; and Keith Smiley, who employed considerable patience as project editor.

I wish to thank my wife, Charlotte, for assuring me that this project could be completed, and Barbara Snowdon, whose reviewing and typing of the manuscript several times made her a West Coast expert on the subject.

It is standard procedure to state that all the errors and omissions are mine alone; however, I would be willing to share them with anyone else as well!

Larry E. Burgess
Redlands, California
March 1980

The story of Mohonk really begins in Maine. March of 1828 was typically cold, snowbound, and windy. But for Daniel Smiley and his wife, Phoebe, the Maine winter was the least of their concerns. During the evening of March 17, Phoebe had given birth to identical twin boys. While Quaker Smiley was not given to celebrating St. Patrick's Day, the new additions to his family made March 17 something of a "Smiley day" for Daniel, his family, and friends in Kennebec County.

Daniel and Phoebe Smiley had their two boys recorded in the Quaker Meeting in Vassalboro as Alfred Homans and Albert Keith Smiley. Ancestry had provided the twin brothers with a Scottish inheritance from their father and English Puritan from their mother.

From their first days in school, the Smiley brothers' identical appearance confused teacher and friend alike. Even their mother had difficulty in telling Alfred from Albert. Albert recalled that when "brother and I were born we were so much alike that our mother tied ribbons on either our arms or legs, I do not remember which, to identify us." Albert also recalled that he and Alfred always worked together, walked together, slept together, had measles, mumps, and whooping cough together. Nor had they a separate article of clothing or money between them until they were forced to divide their possessions when Alfred was married at age twenty-seven. "In the morning," mused Albert in later years, "we jumped into the first suit of clothes that came our way, no matter who wore it the day before." All of their school study and reading was done from one set of books and was done simultaneously. The world of the youthful Smiley brothers was not one of "mine" but rather "ours."

The Smiley twins graduated from Oak Grove Seminary in 1845 and had intended to enter Haverford College, a Quaker school thirteen miles from Philadelphia. Since Haverford was temporarily closed at that time, they both entered the senior class when the college reopened in 1848. The twins graduated in 1849. In the meantime they had been hired by the college as instructors.

Their home in Maine had inculcated them with an appreciation for education, a respect for hard work, and an ability for making friendships and for companionship. More importantly, Alfred's and Albert's parents had imbued them with a firm conviction and vibrant belief in the Quaker reverence for life. Upon leaving Vassalboro for Haverford, the Smileys brought to their college experience a profound appreciation for nature, a respect for the interrelationship between people and their environment, and a recognition of the importance of beauty in daily life. They left Haverford trained with the tools of scholarship. They came to the world imbued with a sense of mission and stewardship; they came identical in resemblance, united in purpose. This background would translate into a remarkable and unique business.

(Opposite) The Smiley Twins, Alfred and Albert, Founders of Mohonk.

After a career in teaching, Albert became principal of Friends School (now called Moses Brown School) in Providence, Rhode Island. Alfred, as co-principal, later moved his family to a farm in Poughkeepsie, New York, which he had purchased in order to provide a suitable environment for his wife and six children. The farm venture was another enterprise that Alfred and Albert undertook jointly, although Alfred ultimately planned to settle there permanently with his family. Albert owned a little more than half of the 115 acres, while Alfred owned the farm house, the barns, and the other out buildings. "We expected to live there for the rest of our lives . . . . ," Albert was later to observe.

But time and circumstance have a way of altering the best laid plans. When not busy with farming, Alfred delighted in taking his family on long walks and picnics in new places. He knew many interesting facts about nature, acquired over the years of study and teaching. Because of his interesting narratives, family and friends eagerly accompanied Smiley on his walks. As a result of one of Alfred's outings the lives of all his family were never to be the same.

(Above) Friends Boarding School in Providence, Rhode Island, now known as Moses Brown School.

(Opposite) Access route to Mohonk. Lake Shore bridge in 1860's.

Chapter One
An Outing To Paltz Point

*"But in spite of the burnt trees and dreary surroundings of the
little tavern, the lake was there and the rocks and the cliffs and
the making of a fine estate."*

A.K. Smiley, 1907

Having completed the summer's harvest in September of 1869, Alfred Smiley decided to set off on
an outing. A friend, Jacob Haviland, suggested that West Point or a place called Paltz Point would
both be interesting areas to visit. After drawing lots to see where they would go, Smiley, his wife,
daughter Susan, son Edward, sisters Rebecca and Sarah, and friends the Havilands, Underhills,
and Ferrises set out for Paltz Point. The party took a ferry in Poughkeepsie across the Hudson
directly west to Highland, and then drove the horses and surreys up the mountain to the foot of
Paltz Point, not far from the town of New Paltz (a community started in the seventeenth century
by French Huguenot families).

After driving up wooded hillsides and rounding a bend in the road, Alfred Smiley and his party
were confronted with a stunning vista. Before them lay the imprisoned waters of a small lake,
called Mohonk*, surrounded by rugged glaciated rock formations, partially covered by a
heavy growth of trees and shrubs. Alfred and the hardier members of the expedition slowly
struggled up the steep rock path leading to the top of Paltz Point (later renamed Sky Top). Once
on top, the beauties of the area spread out before the eager eyes of the beholders. There, in full
view, lay the still waters of Mohonk and in the distance the surrounding forest. To the east lay the
Wallkill Valley dotted with the checkerboard patterns of farmland; to the west lay the Rondout
Valley and the Catskills; and farther to the south, the rolling hills near West Point with the flatter
land ultimately leading to New York City ninety miles away. In the farthest reaches of their gaze
stretched the lands of five adjacent states.

Alfred at once recognized the numerous possibilities that the lake afforded and believed that it
was the exact spot for the summer home which had been part of Albert's plan for his later years.
He and his companions decided to spend the evening at a tavern located on the northwest shore
of the lake. Smiley engaged Mohonk's owner, John F. Stokes, in conversation concerning
possible sale of the lake. Stokes explained to Smiley that he had purchased the lake in 1858. After
much expense and time he opened up a tavern and on July 4, 1859, he had held a grand opening
celebration. The grand opening was a success, complete with fist fights and "whiskey in plenty."
At present Stokes found himself in financial straits, and the visit by Alfred Smiley could not have
come at a better time.

Alfred Smiley sensed that the splendor of the Shawangunks lay in their individuality, an isolated
range that rose out of cultivated valleys, unlike many eastern mountains, with gradual slopes,
rounded outlines, and broad plateau-like summits. Striking features included precipitous crags,
abrupt, perpendicular and overhanging quartz rock formations. Much of this "Shongum grit,"
Alfred observed, was covered with lichens. It was indeed a magnificent area: folded ridges with

*Legend has it that "Mohonk" means "lake in the sky," but scholars versed in the Delaware Indian tongue feel it was
applied to the white rocks or an area at the base of the mountain.

*(Opposite) Stokes Tavern, the first house at
Mohonk Lake as seen from the northwest.*

(Above) The Stokes Tavern of the 1860's from a Currier & Ives print.

(Above right) From the earliest days Albert Smiley was leader of walks and pointed out natural features of the Shawangunk mountains.

escarpments and crevices; the 2,000-foot Shawangunk ridge thrust out from the Wallkill Valley, revealing magnificent vistas.

All around the lake Alfred could see beauty and the potential for enhancement. Here gleaming quartz crystals shone and olive-colored lichen clusters cast dark patterns; there the glossy green hues of the laurel contrasted with the white stone; all about were hills covered with hardwood foliage, and pine, hemlock, and chestnut.

Though a devastating forest fire in 1864 had left several scars on the trees around Mohonk Lake, Alfred was able to look beyond the unkempt conditions and envision the many possibilities for beautification and ornamentation. The tavern, by comparison one of the finest in the New Paltz area, needed improvements. There was a room for dancing and "people came up from the valley and danced and drank all night." Stokes ran the tavern with the help of an elderly woman cook and an Irish boy. "He sold liquor also, though he tried to keep folk from drinking too much. When people got drunk and hard to manage, Mr. Stokes used to chain them to trees ..." The tavern had ten bedrooms, seven feet by five feet. Each bed was a bunk a foot and a half wide with a straw mattress, one sheet, and one quilt. The room also had one chair, a hen feather pillow and a candle for light. "If anyone wanted to wash, the lake was handy."

That night over dinner, Stokes told Alfred that he had planned to sell the lake and surrounding land to his creditors. Having six children to raise, Alfred was in no financial position to purchase the property from Stokes, but he persuaded the debt-ridden owner to wait until a telegram could be sent to his brother in Providence. "Await a letter and come on immediately," wired the anxious Alfred. Albert, in the midst of a busy time of planning at Friends School for two hundred pupils and eighteen teachers, sent word that he could not make it. Alfred sent another plea and Albert made plans to journey immediately to Paltz Point. Alfred entered into more discussion with Stokes.

Upon his arrival at Mohonk Albert Smiley quickly "fell in love with the scenery and felt sure of its development." Mohonk's environs offered the elixir which he sought. Ever since his wife Eliza's breakdown in health following their daughter Nettie's death in March 1863, Albert had been on the lookout for such a location. About the time of Alfred's fateful excursion, Albert noted, "I, too, suffered as severe a case of nervous prostration as I have ever known," brought about by overwork at school.

Stokes asked $40,000 for the three hundred acres of land and the lake. Albert left instructions with his brother, before heading back to Providence, urging him to bargain with Stokes. Alfred succeeded in persuading Stokes to lower the price, and the two men agreed upon the sum of $28,000. Albert had $14,000 in savings, the result of twenty years' frugality. Included in the $14,000 was $300 that Eliza Smiley had saved while teaching at Friends School. He borrowed the remaining $14,000 and as a result stayed on at Providence to pay his debt. "My sole purpose," stated Smiley, "was to provide a home, and in order to pay for it I started in a business for which, above all things in the world, I had a distaste, and no experience."

At forty-one years of age Alfred and Albert engaged upon an enterprise in resort ownership that was totally foreign to their upbringing and inclination. "I had no more thought of it than going to the moon," observed Albert. Fortunately, Alfred Smiley was nearby in Poughkeepsie on the farm. The proximity of the farm to Mohonk enabled Albert to stay at Friends School and draw a salary in order to meet the expense of fashioning the Mohonk Mountain House and grounds.

Fate or destiny often works in wondrous ways but the potential is sensed and grasped only by those prescient enough to dare. And so, Albert Smiley, school administrator, purchased a lake, a tavern, and some rugged terrain. Mohonk afforded the possibility of a retreat and a business. Plans for a projected hotel must be laid; the land must be scrutinized and roads and paths on the property built to permit access to its beauty.

Frederick Partington in *The Story of Mohonk** captured Alfred's emotions: "To the man who had just climbed the mountain and stood enraptured on the other side of the lake, it was a prospect for which he could imagine no bounds. He saw in that quick sweep of his eye the whole future of the place unfolding and forming. He could scarcely believe that business sagacity had thus far missed a chance like this. He was standing less than a hundred miles from the metropolis of the country; he was surrounded by romantic natural features absolutely unknown to the great outside world—and so unique in character that they could be brought into no comparison with any other known region of the eastern states."

(Top) An aerial view taken in 1928 shows the topography of the mountain range which surrounds Mohonk House, lake and gardens. (Photo by Fairchild Aerial Surveys.)

(Bottom) Sky Top Cliff, known for 200 years as Paltz Point, marked the southwest corner of the patent which the Huguenot founders of New Paltz received from Governor Andros.

*Frederick Partington wrote *The Story of Mohonk* in 1911. An educator and good family friend of the Smileys, Partington had planned to re-write his story when he died in 1924. Subsequent editions retained the original Partington text with updated additions by later Smileys. Other quotations from Partington's book will appear frequently throughout the text.

Chapter Two
Creating The Mountain House

*". . . He and I always thought alike . . . We had many of our
interests in common."*
        A.K. Smiley, speaking of his brother Alfred.

The wisest decision Albert made was to induce his twin brother to oversee the operation at
Mohonk and manage it until a permanent move could be made from Providence. Alfred Smiley
lived in Poughkeepsie, less than twenty miles from Mohonk. He possessed sound business sense,
and complemented his brother well.

During the winter and spring of 1870 the tavern was remodeled to accommodate forty guests.
Verandas were added, roads and paths were surveyed and cut in the forest; the Mohonk
Mountain House was ready for occupancy on June 1st.

William Burgess, hired by Alfred to be the first manager of the Mohonk Mountain House,
proved inept for the job. Lamenting this fact, Alfred observed that Burgess "knew very little about
running a hotel and in those days a hotel man was hardly considered respectable." Respectable or
not, Alfred became resigned to personnel eccentricities and saw to the steady improvement of the
guest facilities. Albert meanwhile determined that Alfred should manage the next year, thus
beginning an association and family involvement which were to grow in future years.

One of the most demanding projects for 1870 was the improvement of the road along the shore of
the lake. Tree stumps had been used as a water fill for the roadbed, but after many decades, as
they rotted, holes developed. Although it was slow in growth and often incomplete, the creation
of the Mohonk resort, and especially the "Mohonk spirit," was similar to the even slower
formation of the Shawangunks themselves: plans, ideas, concepts—molded, tried, and
remolded—eventually fused and like stone conglomerate, were ready to withstand the vicissitudes
of the world and determined to persevere.

The first forty guests at the Mountain House were nearly all personal friends from Philadelphia
and New York. Albert loved to have his friends around him, and they delighted in the
opportunity of spending a summer in such a beautiful place with congenial company. The simple
quarters were soon filled, even though personal friends were at the same time paying guests.

One of the good fortunes was the arrival at Mohonk of Schuyler Colfax, Vice President of the
United States. Colfax, an affable and likeable man, was as yet untouched by his role in the Crédit
Mobilier scandal. From the first Mohonk information circular, April 14, 1870, is this account:
"Vice President Colfax, who visited the place last summer with a party of friends, spoke of it
enthusiastically as reminding him of the wonderful rock and valley views of the Yosemite Valley,
in California, and in a letter addressed to the proprietor, dated Washington, March 27, 1870,
says: 'I was delighted with my visit to Paltz Point (Sky Top), with Mr. Cornell, and regarded the
scenery there as most beautiful and picturesque—far more beautiful, indeed, than I had
anticipated'." This was among the first of many such testimonials which would attract a well-to-
do, educated clientele.

*(Opposite) Albert Smiley conducting morning
prayer service in the old parlor.*

DEED–FULL COVENANT.

John F. Stokes

TO

Albert K. Smiley

Dated ... 18

... County, ss.
Recorded on the ... day
of Nov ... 1869, at 1
o'clock P.M. in Book No. 159
of Deeds, at page 39 0 &c and
examined.

C. W. Deyo, Clerk.

The Smileys decided to run their hotel operation along strictly Quaker lines. The liquor question was an easily determined policy at Mohonk. As Quakers, Alfred and Albert were temperance advocates and so temperance ruled at Mohonk. Stokes urged the brothers to reconsider their decision and suggested that they put in a bar and race track. Without liquor Stokes was certain that the Smileys' venture would lose money and end in defeat. Despite Stokes' doubt and air of local skepticism, the Smileys not only banned alcohol but card playing and dancing as well. Those activities were replaced by a voluntary ten-minute prayer service after breakfast each morning, daily nature walks, lectures, evening concerts, golf (later), bowling, boating, horseback riding, fishing, a church service on Sunday (non-denominational) and an evening hymn-sing, and an emphasis on conversation with others and direct contact with nature.

From the outset the Smileys believed that people should come to the mountains for a respite from the rigors and routine of city life. Why, they asked, engage people in the same activities common in the city? While none of the Mohonk guests were compelled to attend the morning worship service, many did take part. In the early years of Mohonk's development, the Smileys' concern for man's relationship to man and to nature became firmly established. Conversation, quiet, and concerts helped to promote friendships, while nature walks, hikes, and drives encouraged visitors to understand nature more fully. In this way, they fashioned a resort where the guest could feel free from his cares and become invigorated by the bracing air, vivid scenery, and contact with some of the finest minds in America.

For Alfred Smiley the managing of Mohonk proved to be a full-time task. For the first two years he continued to plant his crops on the farm in Poughkeepsie and during the summer he traveled there once a week. Alfred's sons, Edward, Fred, and George, and a hired hand, did most of the farm labor. Finally, he was forced to cease farming in 1872 in order to devote his complete attention to the rapidly expanding business at Mohonk. During the winter of 1872, when Mohonk was closed and when much of the repair work and road construction was taking place, Alfred hired a steward, Colonel James Smith (a brother of William and Andrew Smith of Smith Brothers' cough drop fame) to help in the operations.

Alfred proved to be an excellent manager. While the twin brothers got on well together, Alfred at times became vexed by Albert's lack of business sense. "With all the conclusions to which thee seems to have come I do not at all agree," Alfred admonished Albert in a November 1872 letter. "Whether thee wants to enlarge the number of boarders or not it seems to me *imperatively* needed many better rooms." Urging that Albert realize that profits are large during the season but "the expenses last all the year round," he reminded Albert of the necessity to improve the rooms. Some guests preferred certain rooms while a Mrs. Jones accepted Number 29 *under protest*. Moreover, Alfred noted that an enlargement to the house must be undertaken at once. The final thrust of Alfred's arguments scored the problem: "Next season thee will have all the expenses of a first class house & has had no hesitation about adding expensive kitchen & water closet arrangements & yet does hesitate at the *only point* where an increased revenue may be expected. These matters seem very clear to me and I wonder thee doesn't see them too."

During the decade of the 1870's building and grounds improvement was a priority, with Alfred Smiley favoring the former while Albert pushed for the latter. The house was enlarged in 1871 to accommodate more guests. A telegraph office for the convenience of guests, and especially for the reservations office, was installed in 1873. Increased patronage led to construction of the Dining Room Building in 1874 (in 1893 it would become the Garden Wing until torn down in 1902). The laundry and ice house were enlarged in 1875. A bowling saloon with four alleys was constructed

in 1876; it was used for that recreation until it became the Council house in 1960 (where it presently serves a variety of groups for meetings and religious services). The Rock Building, the oldest existing section of the Mohonk Mountain House, was constructed in 1879. It is a wooden structure built on rock.

Roads, their function and their scenic possibilities, fascinated the Smiley twins. A curve here, a vista there, a sloping descent into a wooded arbor, it did not matter that the straight line is the shortest distance between two points. Fortunately for Mohonk, this unusual blend of aesthetic temperament and skillful use of surveying instruments created a wonderland of carriage roads and paths and trails for walking.

Eagle Cliff Road, long a favorite of hikers at Mohonk, was carved out of "Shongum grit" by horse teams, scraper, and hired men from the nearby Wallkill and Rondout Valleys in 1872. Woodland Drive, running off from Lake Shore Road, reached completion the same year.

The quietude and soft sounds of nature and an opportunity to explore lichen growths on sheer cliffs became a reality with the creation of Undercliff Path in 1874. This path still enables guests to circle the lake and sense an affinity with the poet when he mused, "Are we in the world or is it in us?"

Frederick Partington recounts in vivid style those years when development of the grounds went on with alacrity:

> Wild nature came up to the very doors of the hotel and rough paths or trails had been broken only to prominent points. Not infrequently guests lost their way on the long tramps, and on one occasion a lady despairing of ever getting home became hysterical and set up heart-rending shrieks till help came. She was found standing two hundred feet from the house.

(Opposite) A reproduction of the cover of the original deed.

(Above left) The Minnewaska Mountain Houses, known as the Wildmere (left) and the Cliff House (right), established by twin Alfred H. Smiley.

(Above right) The dining room addition was converted to bedrooms in 1893 and continued in use until its demolition in 1902.

A local advertisement for the first season of Smiley ownership. Opening day was June 1, 1870.

To make accessible the beauty and romance of the mountain, the systematic construction of paths was begun. Through labyrinth and forest, over ravines and under precipices, through fissure and cavern and solemn vales year after year the trails were made and the trails then widened into walks, till one could well nigh spend a summer in tramping without the repetition of a path.

As the amenities of the Mountain House and the striking natural features became more accessible, the reputation of Mohonk was spread by enthusiastic guests. The Smiley brothers did not believe in formal advertising, preferring to have more direct relationship with their guests. For many years word-of-mouth advertising was relied upon. The Lake Mohonk Mountain House brochure was a rare exception, employing printed advertisement. Published yearly, these brochures described the facilities, listed the prices, and contained selected comments—all unsolicited—by former guests or newspapers. Advertising may not have been used officially by the Smileys, yet Alfred's son, Edward, recalls that Albert Leroy stayed in the fall and early winter of 1873 and worked outside, and in January he went to New York and handed out small one-page circulars by ringing doorbells from Canal Street to Central Park.

The 1874 brochure contained brief statements describing the Smiley attitude toward advertising: "From the first opening of the house four years ago, the plan has been steadily continued to employ no correspondents, and never, directly or indirectly, to solicit any newspaper notices whatever." Among the favorable comments were those from a number of prominent people. "Lake Mohonk is one of the most interesting places I have visited," remarked Daniel Huntington, noted artist and president of the National Academy of Design. Arnold Guyot, the first Professor of Geography and Geology at Princeton University, visited Mohonk several times before 1887. It was in that year that his well-known statement was printed in a Mohonk publication: "Few spots on our continent unite so much beauty of scenery, both grand and lovely, within so small a compass, to be enjoyed with so much ease." Dr. Howard Crosby, Chancellor of the University of New York, observed, "You have done a good service in calling public attention to a spot so romantic, so varied in its scenery, so health-invigorating, and withal so accessible; and you have added to the good service by making one's stay at Mohonk so comfortable, I may even say so luxurious."

Such panegyric might appear gratuitous, yet it was genuinely felt and honestly expressed by thousands of satisfied guests as Mohonk continued. By appealing to a specific class of people who shared similar ideals with Mohonk's owners, the Mohonk Mountain House became independent of the rapid changes or fads which frequently swept through society. With such a background of self-imposed protection, the Smileys maintained a paying business and relied on the constant patronage of upperclass families, mostly from the East Coast area. The result was a remarkable blend of forces, social and environmental, that caused Mohonk to gain in reputation as a resort of charm and culture. Though "Mountain House" was a term commonly applied to resort hotels, it took on a special emphasis with the Smileys. At Mohonk guests were made to feel like members of a family in a home. Conversely, guests, like a family, were asked to abide by the Mohonk spirit and the aims of the Smiley family.

A confirmed proponent of the family outing, Alfred Smiley, as Mohonk's manager, had little spare time for such pleasures. In the summer of 1876, however, he arranged to take his family and the Albert Smileys on a picnic to Peterskill Falls, a few miles southwest of Mohonk. The driver of their carriage pointed to the top of a mountain towering above the Peterskill and told them of a lake on top. The lake was called Coxing (originally spelled Coxen); the driver offered to show the group the path leading to the top. Alfred, his sons, and Albert readily accepted the driver's offer and the party followed him up a rocky, narrow pathway. Upon reaching the top of the mountain Alfred and his sons and Albert beheld a magnificent setting. There lay a lake, somewhat larger than Mohonk, with sparkling water the color of lapis lazuli. The rock cliffs surrounding the lake were striking and sheer, intermittently covered with thick foliage. In order to obtain a better perspective, Alfred climbed a tree to see what the outlook presented. The view was similar to that to be seen from Mohonk, and Sky Top could be seen seven miles to the north.

Alfred immediately inquired as to the owner of Coxing Pond and found that it belonged to George Davis, who lived not far away in a village called the Trapps. After traveling the two miles from Coxing Pond to the Trapps, Smiley stopped on his way home to see Davis and planned to inquire if the lake were for sale. Davis was willing to sell the property and Smiley arranged that Davis should purchase all the additional land bordering the lake that he did not already own. After this request had been accomplished, Smiley bought approximately 2,500 acres of land in the first of a series of acquisitions. With Coxing Pond in his possession Alfred Smiley planned to create his own mountain retreat.

After his purchase of additional acreage, Alfred decided that such a beautiful spot required a better name than Coxing Pond. He renamed the lake in the Indian tradition, "Minnewaska." During the latter part of 1876 he planned the first stages of his hotel and grounds development. Before construction could begin on the hotel building, Alfred had to build a road up to Minnewaska. As in Mohonk's case, all of the lumber and equipment had to be taken up the mountain on a steep, rocky road. The actual construction of the mountain house began in the fall of 1877. In the spring of 1878 the Alfred Smiley family moved out of the Mohonk House and into the nearly completed Minnewaska Mountain House.

Alfred continued to serve as business manager at Mohonk and during the busy summers of 1877-79 he drove his horse and buggy between Mohonk and Minnewaska daily. Such burdens were borne out of a continuing agreement in purpose nurtured by the twin brothers. On June 14, 1879, a large bell ringing in its tower announced that the Minnewaska Mountain House was open officially for business. Alfred suggested that Albert had better soon seek a new manager for Mohonk.

Albert saw construction completed on the new building of wood built on rock at the Mohonk House called the Rock Building, resigned his position as principal of Friends School in the last part of 1879, and moved permanently to Lake Mohonk. Alfred then became free to devote his full attention to the Minnewaska estate, eventually to consist of 10,000 acres.*

From 1879 when the Old Minnewaska Road was constructed, and especially after the building of Minnewaska Road in 1907, horseback riders and carriages traveled between the two resorts. For a considerable time there was complete reciprocity for guests of one place taking meals at the other, in connection with those regular carriage trips between the adjoining properties. By the early 1960's economic factors, including the sale of Minnewaska and lack of demand for carriage rides of such a distance, brought that era to a close.

This Mohonk House parlor was used for lectures, religious services, music, and games. It was replaced in 1899 by the spacious room in the Parlor Wing.

*In 1972, 7,000 acres were purchased by the Nature Conservancy for conveyance to the State of New York. This land became Minnewaska State Park. In January 1978 one of the two resort buildings, the Cliff House, burned, leaving the Wildmere House and 3,000 acres of land. This property continued under the ownership of Kenneth B. Phillips, who had purchased the Minnewaska Mountain Houses and the entire property from Alfred Fletcher Smiley in 1956.

Chapter Three
Another Brother And A Change For Mohonk

*"He is twenty-seven years my junior and alway seems to me
more like a son than a brother."*
    A.K. Smiley, speaking of his half-brother Daniel.

Two events occurred in 1879 which would permanently influence the future of Mohonk: the decision of Albert to offer his younger brother a position in the business, thus selecting a successor, and Smiley's appointment by President Rutherford B. Hayes as a member of the United States Board of Indian Commissioners.

Daniel Smiley was born in the family home in Vassalboro, Maine, on November 29, 1855. His father Daniel had married Dorcas Hanson after his first wife's death. A half-brother to Alfred and Albert, Daniel was twenty-seven years younger. His early life in Maine bore similarity to that spent by his older brothers. Daniel also did his schoolwork while clearing stones from his father's fields, and that afforded him ample time to master his lessons. "The stones seemed to grow faster than the potatoes which I planted," Daniel later declared. After attending the Oak Grove Seminary across the way from the Smiley farm, he entered Haverford College. Following graduation in 1878, Daniel went to Philadelphia where he served as an instructor and assistant principal at the William Penn Charter School. He instructed students in Latin and Greek. When Albert first suggested a move to Mohonk, Daniel was completing work on a Greek grammar.

It was no easy decision for Daniel to leave his position as a teacher and embark upon a new and unfamiliar life as manager of a resort hotel. After much discussion with his brother, he accepted the invitation to move to Mohonk in June of 1881 when he was twenty-five years of age. Albert and Eliza, without children of their own, came to look upon him as their own son. They were pleased that the younger brother and his family reciprocated their affection and shared their goals. Early in his stay at Mohonk, Daniel demonstrated that his talents were ideally suited to his new environment and that he would provide the business orientation left by Alfred's departure. He became a willing and able partner in the continuing development of Mohonk.

"He is scholarly and honest and I could trust him," remarked Albert when discussing Daniel's talents. "I had him spend the summer before he was married with me," he recalled, "and I used to take a walk with him . . ." The walks turned out to be more than pleasant interludes. Albert was testing Daniel to see whether his younger brother had the taste to lay out a road or spot a scenic view. "'What a pretty place,' he would say," observed Albert, "and I saw he had good judgment of what was good in nature and art." Before he induced Daniel to come to Mohonk Albert had sought the consent of his brother's future wife. "And she has gone in the bargain," noted Albert. Daniel's wife, Effie, became Albert's private secretary and Mohonk's hostess. ". . . When I get in my dotage," concluded Albert in assessing Daniel's role, "he will take my place, and he is taking it rapidly." That remark made by Albert Smiley in 1899 came seven years after he had already given Daniel full charge of Mohonk's operations.

(Opposite) Daniel Smiley joined his brother Albert at Mohonk in 1880 and became general manager. Effie F. Smiley was a supporter and counselor of three generations of Smileys. She arrived with Daniel in 1881 and lived at Mohonk for seventy years.

Daniel's wife, Effie Newell of China, Maine, was an Oak Grove Seminary schoolmate of Daniel's and lent much graciousness to the Mohonk tradition. She provided encouragement and advice to her husband and her brother-in-law.

Once settled at the Mohonk Mountain House in 1881, Daniel arranged to teach at the local academy in New Paltz during the winter. The New Paltz atmosphere exuded its seventeenth century Dutch and French heritage, and the Dutch language was still being taught when Daniel arrived there. ". . . I am happy and glad to have this opportunity to say before you all," Daniel declared in his response at the 1899 dedication of the parlor, "what I do not know that I have ever said to my brother, that I am exceedingly glad for the pleasant experiences and the many, many happy days that I have had here with him." He also noted that he was grateful for Albert's urging him to come to Mohonk. "I think perhaps I can do some good instructing others," said Daniel; "perhaps there is a chance here to satisfy myself in as great an extent as in the professional life." Like Albert, Daniel remained interested and involved in educational work for the rest of his life. His service to a number of college boards of trustees on the East Coast and in the West indicated an intense dedication to his former profession.

As the manager of Mohonk, Daniel Smiley evidenced shrewd business sense. He was forever fostering good relations between Mohonk and its employees. "It has always been our desire to get our employees to understand that they must do a little better this year than last," he remarked. He also pioneered the idea among his employees and his family that since the hotel was away from the city "we must not get 'stuck' in any emergency . . . we have learned to depend on ourselves . . ." Daniel was responsible for making the Mohonk estate self-sufficient in everything from power and heat to soap and food. Daniel's daughter, Ruth, recalled that her "Uncle Albert always wanted things done right now and could not understand why the plants could not grow faster. My father would remind him that all things were accomplished in good time."

With the ability to envision and create like Albert, Daniel also served as a steadying force to his brother's prodigious undertakings. One of his finest qualities was his sense of purpose, his careful stewardship over the land and human relations of Mohonk. He could admire his brother's visions and grand goals and at the same time give careful scrutiny to the necessary details and financial backing for such projects. He was a rare example of the practical and the ideal in harmonious blend. His devotion to the works and ideals of his brother Albert and to the standards set by Alfred was nurtured often at personal loss of time and money. Daniel was the preserver who made it possible for the Smiley philanthropies of ensuing years to exist and for the Mohonk spirit to continue.

(Top) The first Mountain Rest Boarding House was in operation near the site of the Gatehouse. It was first used in 1885 and was destroyed by fire in 1907.

(Bottom) Albert and his brothers never tired of making scenic panoramas more accessible to their guests—whether by balconies on the Mountain House, by observation towers, or by carriage roads with striking vistas.

(Above left) The Office Building as it appeared during the first thirty years. It was replaced by the Parlor Wing in 1899.

(Above right) Cope's Lookout overlooking the Rondout Valley, was the objective of one of the first Mohonk hiking trails.

(Left) A slender wooden observation tower, across from the Sky Top cliffs, was built in 1880 at the point of Eagle Cliff.

Chapter Four
"We'll Discuss It At Mohonk"

"The service of the Lake Mohonk Conferences to the cause of
Indian advancement can hardly be overemphasized."
Loring Benson Priest, 1942

As a member of the Religious Society of Friends (Quakers), Albert Smiley was steeped in a tradition of concern for social problems and their solution. American Quakers were active in the movement for the aboliton of slavery. The Underground Railroad was established with Quaker help. After the Civil War Quakers were instrumental in efforts to aid freedmen. From the earliest Colonial days they had boldly defended the native American Indians' right to a full life. With such a spirit of social activism it is little wonder that Friend Albert Smiley would find it necessary to do his part toward helping less fortunate peoples.

In the winter of 1879 Albert attended the annual meeting of the Board of Indian Commissioners in Washington, D.C. "Charges of corruption were made at that meeting against certain officers of the Indian Bureau by one of the members of the board," he recalled, "and a committee of the board was appointed to investigate them, of which I was made chairman." Careful investigation by him netted evidence against the three men, and Secretary of the Interior Carl Schurz dismissed them from the Indian service. Schurz then called upon the board to investigate the whole Bureau of Indian Affairs. Smiley was again made chairman of the investigating committee. He later recalled that he "inspected the whole Indian Bureau, and particularly its methods of doing business... This is how I came at once to be deeply interested in Indian work."

One aspect of Indian affairs that disturbed Smiley was the lack of coordination in planning among people who sought to solve the "Indian question," as it was then known. The many organizations, public and private, had little or no communication with each other. It had been the practice of the Board of Indian Commissioners to invite once each year the secretaries of all the religious denominations having charge of Indian work to Washington, D.C. For one day in joint session, reports of field work and Indian affairs were discussed. "One short day seemed to me," noted Smiley, "totally insufficient time to thoroughly complete the discussion, and I tried in vain to have the meeting prolonged."

During an inspection tour of the Santee Sioux Agency in Dakota Territory, Smiley found himself frustrated over the difficult conditions for thorough discussions. He announced to a group of colleagues, "We will finish this discussion at Mohonk Lake, next fall." "I invited them all," he later noted, "to meet at Mohonk the ensuing autumn, and promised to have a large gathering to discuss the whole Indian question."

In 1883 invitations to the first annual Lake Mohonk Conference of Friends of the Indian were sent to fifty people, including the Board of Indian Commissioners. The conference met in October as guests of Albert Smiley and his wife. Smiley suggested that the Board of Indian Commissioners could meet officially at the same time. That was a shrewd maneuver because it allowed the Mohonk Conference reports to be printed in the board's subsequent annual reports.

(Opposite) Albert Smiley contemplates a flower from his garden. Gardening contributed to his good health and thus strengthened him for long service in humanitarian causes.

It also made sure that all the commissioners were brought under the recognition and influence of the nation's leading figures in Indian affairs amidst the congenial and beautiful surroundings of Mohonk. Albert considered it a matter of primary urgency "that those representing the Indian cause should arrive at clear and definite conclusions regarding the object to be attained, that the conference should be plainly set before the public in printed form, and as widely circulated as possible."

The conference chairmen were selected by Albert and possessed views generally in line with the host's goals. Yet Albert did not dictate to the conference. By selecting a presiding officer who possessed tact and diplomacy, and who could cut off desultory discussion, Smiley silently guided the conference participants in seeking tangible goals and not spleen-venting charges. As the yearly meetings continued at Mohonk, concepts were formulated and disseminated; the conferences exerted increasingly wide influence. From 1883 to 1916 they played a significant role in the formation of United States Indian policies. Wrote author and Indian affairs scholar Loring Benson Priest, "Out of their sessions came programs which subsequently inspired much criticism, but which then represented the majority thinking of friends of the Indian. The policies they recommended were those which guided administration of Indian affairs during the next quarter century."

The high-minded sentiments and spirited discussions which characterized the conferences were followed by a chance for delegates to relax and mull over the proceedings. The conferences opened their sessions at 10 a.m., adjourned for lunch at noon, and resumed at 8 p.m. after dinner. The early morning was left open for free time and wandering about the estate. The afternoons were often taken up with a longer carriage ride or trip to nearby Minnewaska. So enjoyable was the 1884 journey to Minnewaska that the conference minutes noted that the evening session was late in starting because the delegates did not return from their pleasant trip until after dark. Such a schedule permitted debate without explosive loss of temper arising from overly long sessions.

The Mohonk Indian conferences brought together prominent men and women from all aspects of concern for Indian affairs. Smiley invited secretaries of all the religious societies, the Senate and House Committees on Indian Affairs, army officers having dealings with the Indians, members of the Bureau of Indian Affairs, heads of Indian schools, members of the Indian Rights Association and Women's National Indian Association, leading newspaper editors, and philanthropists. A random sampling of names in attendance at the conferences indicates not only the type of influential delegate but also the fact that many were frequent guests at Mohonk: Generals N.A. Miles, O.O. Howard, Clinton B. Fisk, and John Eaton; publishers Edwin Ginn and Henry O. Houghton; businessmen John Arbuckle, John D. Rockefeller, and Darwin R. James; clergymen Lyman Abbott, Theodore L. Cuyler, Bishop H.B. Whipple, and Cardinal James Gibbons; political and government leaders Charles J. Bonaparte, Senator Henry L. Dawes, former President Rutherford B. Hayes, and Andrew D. White; authors and publishers Samuel June, Isabel Barrows, Edward Everett Hale, and William Hayes Ward; and reformers Samuel C. Armstrong, Alice C. Fletcher, Richard H. Pratt, Amelia S. Quinton, and Herbert Welsh.

After 1890 Indians like Dr. Charles Eastman, Dr. Carlos Montezuma, and Chester Cornelius expressed their opinions and mingled with the members. Often Indian pupils at various schools were guests. A few listed on the membership roles include J. DuBray, Hattie Longwolf, Dennison Wheelock, Samuel George, and Francis LaFlesche.

Members of the Board of Indian Commissioners and their wives with Daniel and Effie Smiley (extreme right and left rear, respectively) in 1921. They continued to meet each fall at Daniel Smiley's invitation for a number of years after the termination of the larger conferences.

When the chairman rang his "five-minute bell" for the last time at the 1916 Lake Mohonk Conference, it marked the end of a thirty-three year campaign by Mohonk for reform in Indian affairs. As a personal effort, the conferences reflect, through their records and reports, the unselfish and dedicated humanitarianism of Albert and Daniel Smiley. As a public event, the conferences represent the coalition of a remarkable and diverse group of influential men and women into a unified whole. The Smileys and hundreds of participants strove at Mohonk to secure a better life for the Indians. They sought to create an "Indian American," a citizen and a partner in society.

Just as millions of European immigrants with many diverse cultures and languages had been Americanized in the "melting pot," it seemed natural that the Indian, too, should be assimilated. To Smiley and his associates, it seemed wrong for the United States to segregate Indians on reservations, to deny them citizenship and, above all, to prevent them from sharing in the American culture.

It would be incorrect, however, to suppose that the Mohonk spirit was nothing more than an exaggerated ethnocentrism condescending to raise the members of an inferior culture to civilized standards. A careful reading of the thirty-four conference reports reveals not only deep compassion and a drive for equality of opportunity and civil rights, but also, at least after the turn of the century, a desire to continue in the Indian an appreciation of his native arts and handicrafts.

The campus of Haverford College in 1910 where the reports and records of the Mohonk Conferences of Friends of the Indian are now located in the library.

Mohonk's efforts were unflagging. Charitable funds were solicited at the conferences to pay for legal protection for the Mission Indians, the Pueblos, the Pimas, and the Alaskan natives. Some of the Mohonk guests provided scholarships to send young Indians to college. The conferences underwrote the "Mohonk Lodge" at Colony, Oklahoma, and the pottery works at Laguna, New Mexico, both of which provided direct educational, cultural, and medical benefits for the Indians. Much of the support of these projects came from Mohonk.

Subsequent events proved the policies advocated at Mohonk to be a mixture of success and failure. As an influential group seeking to arouse public and governmental conscience the conferences were an unqualified success. But after seeking the formal adoption of many of the changes that it had advocated, Mohonk often found itself unable to see to the practical implementation of its theories.

Hopes for sound health, equality of opportunity, and full civil rights stood little chance of fulfillment in the face of political and private resistance to execution of the laws. The political mischief that afflicted the Indian Bureau—admitted by the commissioners and condemned by the crusaders—served to weaken the thrust of Mohonk's reforms. Moreover, looking back from our own perspective, we see that some of the reform solutions that it advocated were impracticable; certain liberal or avant-garde positions of 1905 have become today's quaint, outmoded notions.

But the work of the Lake Mohonk Conferences has left an enduring legacy worthy of study. In 1883 the predominant tendency of the nation was to ignore or exterminate the Indians. By 1916 the attitude of the public and the Government alike had been dramatically altered. Serious concern for education, health, and preparation for citizenship had replaced persecution. Compassion and understanding had begun to supplant indifference and hostility. While treatment of the Indians remains a blot on our national reputation, a study of the Mohonk conferences reveals that during the period between 1883 and 1916 Albert and Daniel Smiley did much to change and bring about improvement of the treatment of the Indians. The name "Mohonk" became known throughout the land. In the 1960's the Smiley family transferred the 22,000 items of Indian Conference records to Haverford College, where they are now utilized by researchers and students of American history.

(Opposite) In October 1899 the members of the Lake Mohonk Conference of Friends of the Indian assembled for their picture outside their new meeting room in the Mohonk parlor, officially opened just in time for this conference.

Chapter Five
"Thistle Pluckers And Rose Planters"

"I have treated this property, the result of seventy-six purchases, as a landscape artist does his canvas, only my canvas covers seven square miles."

A.K. Smiley, 1907

Albert and Daniel Smiley worked long and hard during the 1880's and 1890's not only to fashion a Mohonk spirit but also to blend the handiwork of nature with the handiwork of people. Daniel, especially after 1890 when he assumed the management of the Mohonk operation, proved to be a *rara avis* by having the ability of the engineer and the creativity of the artist. As Daniel Smiley, Daniel's grandson, points out, "Mohonk forestry goes back almost to the beginning of scientific forest management in the United States." In the 1900's Albert Smiley would tell his guests that over a thousand cords of wood were cut annually from four square miles of Mohonk forest for the "benefit of the woods." In 1877 Guyot's Hill and Prospect Hill were buckwheat fields. "Most of the trees on those hills were set out by us and are the result of careful forestry," Albert proudly proclaimed.

This thrust of aesthetics stemmed from the Smileys' concern that visitors to Mohonk be challenged to heighten their perceptions of nature and people's relationship to it. This appreciation for natural beauty drew much of their effort into the area of "aesthetic forestry." "Through the years," writes A. Keith Smiley, "there has ever been the desire to manage our woodlands so as to attain more than one benefit, while making use of the latest forestry techniques."

Albert and Daniel, along with their successors, closely supervised the cutting of views along the more than sixty miles of roads and trails. For example, a vista of the Trapps might be framed by a gnarled tree trunk and colorful foliage. In less accessible wooded areas the emphasis was placed on a long-range yield of wood for a variety of uses: red oak for furniture (made on the property), plank for road bridges, Christmas trees, wood for fireplaces, poles for the railings, red cedar posts for the Mohonk farm fences, and ash logs to sell for baseball bats.

"I never take a walk or drive over the estate, but I find some ugly tree to be removed, a new path to be built, a group of trees or shrubs to be set out, a vista to be opened, groups of trees to be planted to give seclusion to a too open view, a summerhouse to be built, bright flowers to be set out or dead flowers to be removed," Albert Smiley declared in a statement summarizing the impetus of Mohonk's 7,500-acre landscaping plan.

A 1965 essay in the weekly *Mohonk Bulletin* provides insight into the latest purported phase of aesthetic forestry undertaken by the Smiley family. Wrote Virginia Smiley, "At various times during its tenure at Mohonk the Smiley family has been questioned concerning its part in such major projects as the artistic arrangement of the rocks in the Labyrinth across the Lake, and the removal of all the dead laurel blossoms on the property. Our answer is a simple denial of responsibility."

(Above) The log cabin on Mossy Brook Road was originally built by Huguenot settlers about 1771. It is the oldest building on Mohonk lands.

(Opposite) The carriage drive to Memorial Tower passes Whittier Outlook at the southern end of the Sky Top ridge.

Washington's Profile as seen from a vantage point near Sky Top Path. The escarpments of The Trapps and Millbrook Mountain are silhouetted against the southern horizon.

She suggests rather the more challenging question of dead trees which to the casual observer might be considered aesthetically displeasing. But 7,500 acres made removal impossible, except where danger might arise along roads or paths:

> *To an ecologist a dead tree, whether it be standing or lying under a blanket of moss, is just as beautiful as a sprouting seedling or a living tree in full autumn color. Each state of growth and decay is a part of the tree's destiny, and has a beauty which may only become evident when one is conscious of it as a step in the cycle of life, death, and rebirth. Is it possible that, through a gain in understanding and appreciation of the natural processes, we searching humans might grow in our relation to the seven ages of man?*

For Albert Smiley the formal flower gardens at Mohonk held a special place in mind and heart. The entire family came to appreciate—and even indulge—"A.K." in these gardens. "Thee may charge it to the flower garden" became the byword among the family. Other departments were held closely accountable for expenses, but the Mohonk gardens were and are evaluated along the lines of pleasure, satisfaction, good health, beauty—but not in dollars. Daniel's son, Albert K., Jr., named for his uncle, especially favored roses—and lots of them. Today at Mohonk the battle between roving and ravenous deer who prefer roses for dessert and the high cost of labor still permits a memorial rose garden to bloom in his memory.

The travail and difficulty in planting and caring for the Mohonk gardens, renowned nationwide by afficionados, is best described by Frederick Partington in 1911:

> The demolition of the old stables in 1888 marked the real beginning of the extensive gardens. The land thus liberated grew rapidly larger, and, as already mentioned, no one who has not seen the untamable jungle beyond this point could appreciate the combined enthusiasm and energy required to transform all that into the blossoming acres that now stretch almost to the crest of the mountain. What that garden yields in variety and color, what it succeeds in producing against apparently natural obstacles, is a story by itself.

> No words can convey any conception of the difficulties that confronted the new owner of Mohonk when he really began to exploit the mountains for roads and flower beds. Gardening, with Mr. Smiley, was dangerously near a passion. As nature had arranged things at Mohonk there seemed to be only two places for growing flowers—on the quartz rocks and on the branches of trees. A remote third might have been on the lake—a floating garden. There was not a square of a hundred feet where anything but ferns and lichens could hold on—and it had taken some of the lichens a hundred years or more to cover a few inches. The old guests with records of thirty summers are the only ones who can really appreciate the miracle of the gardens. They can look back to the time when Mr. Smiley used to point with pride to a bed of geraniums on the side of the road close to the water and to a delicate white birch tree that looked like a frail child—not long for this world. He succeeded in stringing those geraniums along the road as it swings over the bridge and to the south, and every bud cost him, probably, five dollars. Anybody caught plucking one would doubtlessly have paid or have been sent away. He classed that sin with drink. Gradually these ganglia of flowers began to grow. Larger beds were made—soil was brought long distances and all around the exterior of the house plants were made to flourish in especially fortified enclosures and in soil that practically had to be renewed to the last particle every year. Finally when the old stables near the bowling alleys were removed in 1888 the present garden, as already noted, began its remarkable expansion. Beyond the stables lay a wilderness of boulders and cliffs. To civilize this was literally asking Faith to remove mountains. It was done partly, perhaps, to provide space for flowers. It was more likely that the impossible nature of the task acted as a challenge. It is always so with intrepid engineers—pole seekers—besiegers. Getting the land may have been the hardest thing Mr. Smiley ever did—but taming it gave him the greatest delight of his life. He did not rest until he had coaxed into blossom nearly twenty acres of that hopeless slope of the mountain. Most of the earth was brought a mile or more—and the wonder is, still, how it is ever kept in place. To this garden Mr. Smiley has given no end of time and intelligent care, and his reward has been, as he himself says, "a long life and abounding health."

Now "completed," the Mohonk gardens afford guests and visitors an array of blooming flowers—marigolds, peonies, phlox, heliotrope, pansies (the twins' favorite), herbaceous perennials and shrubs—amidst a sweep of green lawn criss-crossed with arbors, trellises, paths, benches, and summerhouses.

Protecting the Mohonk property became one of the great challenges confronting Mohonk's founders and continues to be such today (more will be said of this later). The original purchase in

The Flower Gardens in the 1930's.

(Left) Early methods of loading shale for road surfacing were "labor intensive".

(Top) Clearing the way for building a carriage road.

(Bottom) The road begins to take shape while two guests watch the rock-drilling.

1869 was for approximately 300 acres, and it included the lake, the tennis court area, a narrow strip along Eagle Cliff, some of Home Farm, and Sky Top, and ended in the garden near the greenhouse.

It became readily apparent from the beginning that encroachments from neighbors and from those who did not share in the goals of Mohonk must be dealt with. Self-protection became an underlying policy of Mohonk. Lacking the necessary governmental impetus (and recall that conservation became a "noble alternative" only under Theodore Roosevelt's administration), the Smileys had to "go it alone."

Again as Partington recounts:

> In the first place, neighbors in the country do not always share your respect for natural scenery and natural objects . . . To protect Mohonk from dangers, Mr. Smiley began a series of purchases. He was surrounded by farms, and one after another they were added to his holdings. "The hardest work I ever did in my life," said Mr. Smiley, "was the buying of those farms." No sooner was a menace disposed of in one direction than another one appeared somewhere else. It was a perennial contest. Farms good, bad and indifferent had to be gathered in . . . . It has taken over one hundred distinct purchases to establish the present state of immunity.

Spring Path skirts the Labyrinth, a jumble of rocks which provides a challenging route to Sky Top for those who enjoy rough terrain.

The Mountain House Takes Shape

"I take great pleasure in opening this parlor . . . . We have needed
this room for years, especially for our conferences. We have been
expecting to do it all along and now we have a room that will
seat four hundred people . . . ."

Albert Smiley, at the dedication of the
new Parlor, 1899

The growing list of guests who patronized Mohonk year after year, who "talked it up" among their friends, as well as the demands of the Indian Conferences, necessitated expansion and improvement of the Mountain House. In 1887-88 the Central Building was constructed with N. LeBrun and Sons in New York City designing the structure. Four years later the Grove Building, the present dining room, and the kitchen building were added with LeBrun and Sons again in charge. Woods employed in the main dining room included yellow pine for the floor and white pine for the walls.

The exquisite Stone Building came to fruition in two sections and after great expense. Designed by James E. Ware, a New York City architect, the first section was completed and used in 1899 and the second in 1902. Some of the steel support work on the latter phase was supplied by James McKinney and Son of Albany. Both LeBrun and Ware came to Mohonk with impressive credentials. LeBrun had designed many well-known churches in New York City and the Metropolitan Life Insurance Company tower which received the medal of honor from the American Institute of Architects. James E. Ware served as architect of the interior of the Madison Avenue Presbyterian Church and also as creator of Halcyon Hall in Millbrook, New York.

LeBrun and Ware, along with considerable input from Daniel Smiley, fashioned Mohonk Mountain House into a Victorian and Edwardian architectural wonderland that not only thrills both first-time and old-time guests, but also provides ample areas for conversation, strolling, sitting, and even "exploring." Sitting on the west side of the lake, rising seven stories skyward, the Mountain House stretches nearly an eighth of a mile, and is reminiscent of a castle or grand chalet in Europe.

The stepped-up tempo of Mohonk's outreach program called for a larger parlor and a meeting room for programs. Also, a demand for more office space needed to be met. The present Parlor Building, including the new parlor and the office below it (which ultimately became the Lake Lounge), was constructed under the watchful eye of Albert and Daniel Smiley and designed by the then familiar Mohonk architect, James E. Ware. With a view of the cliffs and Sky Top, the new parlor became the center for the cultural and philanthropic activities of the Smiley family. Outside porches with balustrades and millwork of yellow pine complemented the interior parlor trim of birch stained the color of mahogany. The floor of the office below was constructed of oak while the paneling was of chestnut.

The unique relationship between Mohonk's guests and its owners often occasioned wry comments upon various things. Thomas G. Ritch, a Mohonk "perennial", noted that the makeup of the guests, coming as they did from metropolitan areas, often was starkly opposite to the attitudes and philosophy found at Mohonk. Discussing a friend's city habits which were cleansed by a stay at Mohonk, Mr. Ritch notes, "He might have lived longer if he had spent less time in

(Opposite) The present Mohonk Parlor, scene of many gatherings of distinguished persons and of countless programs of fine music, inspirational talks, and lectures.

(Top) The Mountain House as it appeared 1888-1898 prior to construction of the Stone Building and the Parlor Wing.

(Bottom) The first lawn tennis "grounds" were built in 1883, just west of the Grove Building.

New York and more at Mohonk." He also observed that so many city dwellers were attracted to Mohonk because of "quiet and freedom," "a change from city odors to ferns, roses and pines," and "the congenial friendship to which the Mohonk life gives birth."

Lyman Abbott, renowned Congregational clergyman and editor, wrote a delightful account of skepticism often encountered about the Mohonk operation. The story took place in Redlands, California when the Smileys resided there.

Tourist: "What a beautiful place. Who does it belong to?"
Driver: "A.K. Smiley."
Tourist: "It must have cost a lot. How did he make his money?"
Driver: "By a queer kind of hotel in New York."
Tourist: "What kind of hotel?"
Driver: "Well, he didn't have a bar or allow any wine to be served on the table; they didn't allow card playing, or dancing in the parlor; guests were not received nor taken away on Sunday; they have family prayers in the parlor every morning and church services on Sunday."
Tourist: "Where in hell can they get patrons for such a hotel?"
Driver: "They don't get their patrons from that region."

The completion of the Parlor Wing occasioned a dedication exercise. The evening ceremonies on September 26, 1899, were called to order by Albert Smiley. While space does not permit an account of the entire proceedings, Smiley's remarks, mingled with good humor and wry observations, provide a fine insight into "The Mohonk Spirit"—the unwritten code of that period. The spirit itself has modified with changing times, but is the skein which connects and intertwines Mohonk's past with its future.

Excerpts from Albert's remarks illuminate the Quaker philosophy underlying the "house rules":

The house then was conducted the same as it is now, no dancing and no cards, and services every Sunday. And everyone said it was mad and foolish to try and carry on a hotel business that way, and that nobody but "cranks" would come to it. I expected to lose by it, but we stuck to it, and sometimes we had to be a little severe, often losing important guests because they didn't like the regulation, and we said the world is wide, and they could go to some other place, and we succeeded. We do not allow wine on the table. I do not know that it is such an awful sin to drink wine, but I do know that the drinking habit amongst workmen and the better classes is one of the greatest evils of the country. Many can drink wine without doing any harm. You might use it in your rooms in private, I do not know anything about that, but you cannot use it in any public place in this house. The Vice-President of the United States came here, and he was a man that always had his liquor and needed it maybe, but he only got Apollinarius water.

About Sundays, I think it is a very good thing to have one day of rest. I do not think it is more sacred than any other day, every day should be sacred, and every day is "The Lord's Day." There is one day set apart for religious observance, and we observe it, and we want our help to get a rest, our men and horses, everything gets a rest. We have a quiet Sunday, a very unusual thing for a large hotel, and there are many people who appreciate it, as is shown by their coming here.

The large public porches, overhanging the lake, were a feature of the Parlor Wing (1899), providing natural air conditioning by breezes funneling between the cliffs.

(Above) Boating on the Lake was one of the earliest Mohonk activities.

(Above Right) The seven-storied Stone Building was the last major addition to the Mountain House.

(Lower Right) Flat-bottomed row boats combined safety and durability for boating parties in the 1890's.

I should play cards if I was alone, and I think I should play every night, and I think I would like it. I play dominoes every night, and I do not know, but I think I should like cards better. It is the best game there is, except golf. They play cards in the hotels in San Francisco, and they play on Sunday, and that is why we do not have cards here. Young men come here, and they may do it in their rooms, but we do not allow it in the parlors.

I do not know how to dance, but I think I should like it. If we could have dancing in the old fashioned way, square dancing, I think we should have it. A great many people object to dancing, and this house is planned for that class of people, who object to the usual frivolities of hotel life, and we run this hotel on that principle. I am not strict on any one of these lines, but I think it is best for the house, and we intend to follow those lines.

In place of cards, dancing and tippling, we have put before our guests something more desirable, that is a library of good standard works. We were the first house in the country that had a library and all the standard periodicals; we set the ball in motion.

We try to get good books for the guests, and we have entertainments and lectures, and tableaux, charades, etc., and we have a garden of the choicest selection of herbaceous plants in the state. We have spent large sums of money in roads and paths, and we have one hundred and thirty-seven summerhouses, and a large number of settees and seats to entice people out of doors to get enjoyment. We have spent more money than any hotel in the world on roads; the only hotel that in any way approaches us in that respect is the Hotel Monterey, California. We do these things because we want the cultivated . . . classes of people.

The main dining room, with its high ceiling and clerestory windows came into use in 1893. It was enlarged to include the west circle in 1910.

Chapter Seven
Another Conference: Seeking A Peaceful World

*"It would be most deplorable if this house should ever acquire the
mercenary spirit and make the accumulation of money without
higher ulterior aims the goal of its ambition."*
A.K. Smiley, dedication of the Testimonial Gateway,
October 14, 1908

"It was a happy thought and has yielded rich fruitage," observed Smiley family friend, the
Reverend Dr. Theodore L. Cuyler, in assessing the role of the Lake Mohonk Conferences on
International Arbitration begun in 1895.

Albert Smiley's determination to host yearly conferences on arbitration, despite the wrath and
scoffing he might incur from some circles, came from the strongly held conviction that the forces
favoring international arbitration of disputes among nations should unify their ranks.

As a Quaker, Smiley had long cultivated a desire to seek peace rather than wage war, to arbitrate
rather than dictate. He was "impressed in the duty of intelligent and organized propaganda for
the attainment of international peace through arbitration." It was in June 1895 that Smiley called
the first Mohonk Conference on International Arbitration. The time for such a gathering was in
many respects ripe. The United States had been involved in encouraging arbitration of disputes in
one form or another since 1876.

As historian Laurence M. Hauptman has noted,* the Mohonk Arbitration Conferences

> *have been credited with having given impetus to the Hague Conference movement; the
> formation of the big-money peace establishment—the World Peace Foundation and
> the Carnegie Endowment for International Peace—as well as reconstituting an older
> one, the New York Peace Society; the creation of the American Society of
> International Law; and the League to Enforce Peace. Historians, contemporary
> observers and participants have maintained that, besides contributing to the
> movement for international arbitration, the conferences spawned a furthering of
> world peace and international understanding, Pan-Americana, Anglo-American
> amity, and even a version of "Pax Americana." In addition to these interpretations, the
> conferences served one more fundamental and far-reaching purpose: they were the
> harbinger and prototype of the modern American foreign policy "think-tank"; the
> forerunner of such prominent organizations as the Foreign Policy Association and the
> Council on Foreign Relations. Originating during a decisive period in America's
> foreign relations, these international forums were the "first publicly organized elite
> groups in the United States for the regular dissemination of information about broad
> issues of foreign affairs and the theoretical discussion of foreign policy.*

Albert Smiley and dozens of his personally invited guests at the Mohonk Conferences believed
that the earlier attempts at arbitration were but the groundwork for the successful and permanent
implementation of arbitration as a substitute for war. What better country was there to lead in
the support of arbitration, the conference delegates asked themselves, than the United States of
America?

*Introduction to *Index of the Proceedings of the Lake Mohonk Conferences on International Arbitration,
1895-1916* (New York: Clearwater Publishing Co., 1976).

*(Opposite) Members of the Lake Mohonk
Conference on International Arbitration, at
the eleventh annual session held in May 1905.*

The Mohonk Conferences on International Arbitration were not peace conferences. At the first session of the initial gathering in 1895, Albert Smiley described his aims in calling the conference. The report of that year summarizes his statement in this fashion: He asked that "the discussion might not go into the subject of the horrors of war or of the doctrine of 'peace at all hazards,' but might be turned to the consideration of the means by which our own country might have all her disputes with foreign lands settled by arbitration, and might bring other nations to join her as rapidly as possible . . ."

The most powerful and far-reaching address delivered at the 1895 gathering was by the noted author Edward Everett Hale. "A permanent tribunal," he cried to the enthralled attenders, "I want us to urge first, second, last and always a permanent tribunal. That is the thing . . . which must be rubbed into the public mind." Hale's call at Mohonk for a court of permanent arbitration antedated the Hague Conferences by four years and occurred a full twelve years before Elihu Root laid down its implementation as "a chief duty upon the American delegation to the Second Hague Peace Conference to propose such a tribunal."

In 1896, the New York Bar Association had anticipated such a plan, and many of its members (who were participants in the conferences) submitted to President Grover Cleveland a plan for the constitution of a permanent court of arbitration. That plan was also given to Andrew D. White, who was later America's first chief representative at the Hague Conference in 1899. White suggested various concepts and plans that had been discussed at Mohonk during the Hague deliberations. The soft-spoken White, who was a founder and first president of Cornell University and had served in the diplomatic service in Germany and Russia, was one of Mohonk's most enthusiastic supporters.

Among the hundreds of well-known people who attended the conferences between 1895 and 1916 were these: Henry Demarest Lloyd, author; Baron Takahire of Japan; Wu-Ting-Fang of China; Senator Jim Gamboa of Mexico; Professor J. Rendel Harris of England; British Ambassador James Bryce; F.W. Holls, Secretary of the American delegation at the 1899 Hague Conference; Cardinal James Gibbons of New York; Robert Lansing, later Secretary of State under President Woodrow Wilson; Robert Treat Paine, President of the American Peace Society; William Jennings Bryan, Democratic presidential nominee and later Secretary of State under Wilson; William Howard Taft, President of the United States; Elihu Root, Secretary of State under Theodore Roosevelt; and John W. Foster, Secretary of State under Benjamin Harrison. It was through contact and friendship with the Smileys at Mohonk that Andrew Carnegie, businessman and philanthropist, founded The Carnegie Endowment for International Peace, with Albert K. Smiley as one of the original trustees.

One of the peace-making achievements accomplished at Mohonk centered on domestic affairs. The 1916 agenda found former Republican President William H. Taft as presiding officer with William Jennings Bryan, former Democratic presidential candidate, as a featured speaker. These two rivals put on an amiable front but it was noted that during the picture-taking of conference members, they were discreetly placed at some distance from each other!

In the 1960's the Smiley family donated the several thousand documents relating to the Arbitration Conferences to the Swarthmore College Peace Collection. The information contained in these papers provides a useful body of knowledge to those seeking insight into the complicated and delicate nature of international arbitration.

(Opposite) Andrew Carnegie and Albert Smiley have a visit at the Smiley winter home in Redlands, California. Carnegie kept in touch with the proceedings of the Arbitration Conferences but did not attend.

(Above) Undercliff Road formed part of the carriage drive link between Mohonk and Minnewaska. It was one of the Mohonk conference traditions to work in the morning and evening and to have afternoons for recreation. A group carriage excursion to Minnewaska was often included in the program.

Chapter Eight

"Our Guests Are Our Friends"

"Erected by their guests to commemorate the Fiftieth Anniversary of the wedding of Albert Keith Smiley and Eliza Phelps Smiley, the founders of Mohonk, 1857—July 8—1907.
Quaere Monumentum, Circumspice"*

That Mohonk is not the usual hotel is not a revelation to those even distantly acquainted with it. Those who come year after year develop an almost proprietary sense toward the place, and a special feeling of kinship with the Smiley family. This happy condition is a symbiotic relationship which has been carefully nurtured for well over 100 years. For example, the occasion of Albert and Eliza's fiftieth wedding anniversary produced an outpouring of affection rarely witnessed in the annals of guest-host relationships.

Mohonk Lake on Monday, July 8, 1907 was the scene of a celebration honoring Albert and Eliza Smiley on their golden anniversary. Twelve hundred of their friends had made contributions toward the erection of a testimonial Gateway in the Smileys' honor. The Gateway was located on a rise of ground about one and a quarter miles from New Paltz on the eastern edge of the Mohonk estate.

The groundbreaking ceremonies took place in the morning and several addresses were delivered by Smiley friends dealing with events and remembrances of the Smileys' life. In the evening a celebration was held in the Mohonk Parlor, where formal plans for the Gateway construction were presented. John Crosby Brown, a long-time friend of Albert and Eliza, observed in his opening remarks that he had never "acted as treasurer for an object more worthy of recognition than the cause that brings us together tonight . . . and contributions came fluttering to my treasury."

Judge George G. Perkins, secretary of the committee, took his turn in addressing the meeting and humorously described the various suggestions originally offered to honor the Smileys. Some people, he explained, wanted books with notes and a compilation of photographs of Smiley friends and admirers ; others thought a great tower appropriate; while still others preferred oil portraits. "A few went to the length of promising a statue of Mr. Smiley for the garden," commented Perkins. Noting that men of distinction found that personal statues add to the terror of approaching death, he added: "Yet some of us wanted to doom this kindly man to daily embarrassment of meeting himself, face to face, in solemn bronze or marble as he went among his flowers." Perkins concluded by declaring that when someone suggested a gateway "everyone seemed to be pleased with the suggestion . . ." The cost estimate was $20,000 and subscriptions were to be ten dollars apiece.

"The major obstacles we have met with have been Mr. and Mrs. Smiley . . .," added Perkins, "but we have gone resolutely forward . . . not deterred by those we are seeking to honor." Albert Smiley accepted the tributes with characteristic modesty. "Words utterly fail me to express to you, my dear friends, my deep appreciation . . . " He proceeded to name the "four red letter days"

*To seek their monument, look about.

(Opposite) The Testimonial Gateway on the eastern approach to Mohonk via the former stage route. The dedication of the Gateway took place on October 14, 1908.

(Above) This plaque is embedded in the wall above the keystone of the Gateway arch.

(Above left) Eliza Phelps Smiley is described in the first Mohonk history as Albert's "sweet-souled wife." She most certainly would have agreed with the remark that "our guests are our friends."

(Above right) Daniel Smiley's wife, Effie, shared and carried on Albert's concern for the flower garden. She would drive Albert about the grounds on inspection trips.

(Right) By the turn of the century the Old Boys Club had become a Mohonk institution, organizing numerous mid-summer activities.

of his life. The first he said was the study of Latin with Alfred in preparation for college. The second was the first time he met his wife-to-be, Eliza Phelps Cornell. The third day, Smiley suggested, was the discovery of Mohonk and his later purchase of it. He finished by saying, "You all must know that the fourth day is today."

On October 14, 1908, a year after the groundbreaking ceremonies, J. Edward Simmons, chairman of the Gateway Committee, and president of the New York Chamber of Commerce, opened the dedication exercises for the completed Testimonial Gateway. Messages poured in from all over the nation and many were read to the assembled crowd of well-wishers. A final total of 1300 subscriptions had been taken in, totalling about $20,000. Albert Smiley responded to the formal presentation by declaring that: "You could not possibly have made us any gift that would have given us more intense pleasure than this gateway." "You should have seen me drive down five miles every two or three days this summer," he related, "and each time climb up steep ladders, under protest from my family, till finally the topmost story was reached, watching with all the enthusiasm of a boy the huge boulders, weighing many tons each, lifted by steam power and carefully placed in position by skillful masons."

Smiley also related his future plans to lay macadam roads and plant trees and shrubbery around the tower. "We have growing in our nursery house two thousand trees and shrubs ready for planting and are negotiating for more."

In responding to the gift of the gateway, Albert Smiley captured the essence of his hopes for Mohonk and spoke simply but eloquently of its future:

It is most desirable that it should always prove a success as heretofore in its management. Ardently do I desire that a large share of the profits arising from a wise administration of this estate may be used for the good of mankind. I feel sure that the remarkable natural beauty of this large domain will continue to be developed on artistic lines for many ages to come.

In the sunset of life it is an unspeakable gratification that we have a younger brother and his wife who with their children are all interested in maintaining a Christian home where just dealing will prevail, where warm greetings will be extended and kindly interest shown to all. It is a still greater pleasure to feel that for generations to come streams of high-minded, distinguished philanthropists will pass through the portals of this gateway every spring and autumn to discuss great national and international questions which will help to solve some of the great problems of society, and make Mohonk a veritable delectable mountain, known in the remotest corners of the world for its high aims and warm interest in every movement for the betterment of mankind.

(Opposite) A new center for day visitors was opened in 1907. Picnic Lodge offered general merchandise and souvenirs as well as light refreshments.

(Left) The Mohonk Spring House was dedicated in 1904. The ceremony was organized by the Old Boys and included several eloquent speeches.

(Above) The Great Crevice below the point of Sky Top.

Chapter Nine
Transition

*"I am particularly anxious that as a family we shall all pull
together harmoniously. We have strong wills and divided
opinion by inheritance."*
        Daniel Smiley, 1911, Family Conference.

On December 2, 1912, Albert Smiley died peacefully at his winter home in Redlands, California. Eighty-four years of life closed amid success and achievement. It is ironic that unknown to Albert a group of leading American citizens led by the former secretaries of state, John W. Foster and Elihu Root, had placed his name in nomination for the Nobel Peace Prize. Everyone connected with the plan felt sure that had he lived, Albert Smiley would have received the 1913 Prize.*

Man's relation to man and man's relation to nature had become the underpinning of the Mohonk operation. A clientele of sympathetic people, possessed of varied backgrounds, constituted Mohonk's guests. A unique experience in fashioning a harmony between wilderness and the arts of humankind continued to broaden its outreach. Concern for improving the world began to assume different manifestations.

Yet it had not been easy. Money was made abundantly but it was spent abundantly upon house improvements, new roads, new summerhouses, increased conference activities, and nationwide charitable causes.

It may not seem relevant at first blush to the story of Mohonk, but Albert Smiley's philanthropies ranged from coast to coast. Close friends even remarked: "The Smileys made their money at Mohonk and spent it in California." The winter residence in Redlands, California, demanded time, energy, and expense. The gift of a downtown park and library in Redlands, service as a trustee of Pomona College, Brown University, Vassar College, and New Paltz Normal School, all took time—and money. Albert Smiley was not afraid to borrow to see his benefactions enacted because Daniel was there to back his efforts and somehow generate the funds from out of the Mohonk operation.

The property in Redlands, known as Cañon Crest Park or Smiley Heights, was landscaped and kept open for many years for the enjoyment of the public, as a tourist attraction. At a later time, a change in tax policy by the city of Redlands forced the family to close this beautiful park, maintained by them as a benefit to the community.

The use of funds from Mohonk caused Daniel much administrative effort, and not a little worry. He wholeheartedly supported his brother's indefatigable impulses for service and even added to his own burdens by serving on the Board of Trustees of Vassar College, his alma mater Haverford College, and of the University of Redlands, as well as on the Board of Indian Commissioners.

Still, loans needed to be paid, obligations met, and Mohonk's service to guests and employees alike maintained. To the members of his family, Daniel Smiley turned for support. "I suggest that

*The Nobel Committee did not at that time award prizes posthumously.

*(Opposite) Three generations of the Smiley
family, photographed a few years prior to the
death of Albert Smiley.*

(Top) The Greenhouse provides plants for the Garden and for the Mountain House.

(Bottom) In Redlands, California, their winter home, Albert and Daniel helped provide the town with a fine public library.

(Above right) The network of smooth paths and rough trails has gradually increased until it is now possible to walk for many days without repeating a route.

our motto for the family be the one word 'Together'," he told them. He urged them individually and collectively to "live up to its full meaning."

Effie F. Smiley's guidance, sage advice, soothing manners, and ability to deal with vagaries of human nature made her role a key factor in Mohonk's development between 1912 and 1951. She served as hostess owing to the semi-invalid state of Eliza Smiley and brought to that role grace and assurance. As Daniel's wife, she shared with her husband a sense of stewardship over Mohonk. Not "mine" but "ours" became the attitude in expressing the Mohonk responsibilites.

The early 1900's had seen a fast pace in physical improvements to the Mountain House and new roads as well: in 1901 Bonticou Road was extended and the present power plant built; 1903, Undercliff Road was created along a talus slope; also built were Terrace Drive, the golf clubhouse at Mountain Rest, the Artists Lodge; 1904, Bonticou Road again extended and North Lookout Road carved out. In 1907 Picnic Lodge opened and Minnewaska Road was completed. Between 1908 and 1913, a third stage road to New Paltz was built, the dining room circle extension completed, new tennis courts added, the golf course lengthened and improved, a croquet court laid out and the first issue of the *Mohonk Weekly Bulletin* (May 1912) appeared. Cottage Grove, a small colony of houses on the property for supervisors and heads of departments, had been designed to encourage employee family life.

Daniel Smiley's three sons, A.K. Smiley, Jr., named for his uncle, Hugh and Francis G. assisted in the management of the hotel. Hugh became the first editor of the *Bulletin*. His work with the gift shop and furnishings was augmented by his wife, Hester, who helped with the social and entertainment duties. In the early 1920's Hugh left the family business to start his own resort operation in Massachusetts, and while his tenure was comparatively brief, his kindliness with guests, his design of the Laurels residence and his appreciation for Mohonk's tradition helped his father considerably.

Daniel and Effie's daughter, Ruth, during the 1900's became increasingly involved with Mohonk duties. She was the sports director, helped with the Picnic Lodge operation, and frequently accompanied her father as he made his rounds about the property. Ruth later moved to California and was married there, settling on the Redlands property with her family.

A.K. Smiley, or "Bert" as he was known to close friends and family, and Francis ("Doc") became their father's able assistants. Bert Smiley took naturally to the operations end of the family business, while Francis took delight in overseeing the Mohonk farms, engineering problems, and outside improvements, as well as accounting procedures.

One of the inherent qualities of the Smiley family lay in the ability to select spouses who not only served as loving life-partners, but who also lent quality, creativity, and fresh ideas to the Mohonk operation. Bert married Mabel A. Craven, daughter of Mohonk guests and close family friends, John V. and Anna Craven of Pennsylvania. Mr. Craven was a man of wide business experience and an appreciator of Mohonk's two-fold outreach toward people and nature. Mabel lent her guidance to matters of housekeeping and employee relations.

Frank Craven, a brother of Mabel, was associated with Mohonk for a brief period during the time when Mohonk was first developing a fleet of autos and trucks. He was the first to operate the Mountain Rest transfer when guests came in cars, and during those winters served as Mohonk postmaster. He was a beloved friend of many members of the family and staff.

Francis Smiley was no less fortunate in meeting and marrying his wife. In 1915 the Arbitration Conference delegates subscribed funds to purchase a choralcelo, one of the latest innovations in the musical world, a blend of the piano and organ. In 1919 a lovely instrumentalist came to play the choralcelo, Rachel Orcutt from Boston. The mountain was to become her home, for she and Francis were married in 1920. With grace, kindness, and talent as a performer, Rachel added her abilities to the Mountain House's cultural endeavors.

The Club House at the Mountain Rest golf course built in 1903 is one of the oldest golf houses in America.

Chapter Ten
New Challenges

"With great earnestness of purpose, but in all humility,
I accept the heritage."

Daniel Smiley

The sincerity with which Daniel Smiley assumed ownership of Mohonk was real indeed, but so were the challenges confronting him which sought to impede and even curtail certain aspects of Mohonk goals.

The shot at Sarajevo in 1914 proved to be a firebell in the night. Three years later America entered World War I, "the war to end all wars." War was personally objectionable to the Smiley Quaker conscience and the direct effect of it upon Mohonk brought an end to the conferences and produced shock waves upon the business.

Both the Indian and Arbitration Conferences were cancelled for 1917—a decision thought to be temporary, but from which the two enterprises never recovered. Faced with substantial debts, the result of Albert's philanthropies, and the tide of war which had thrown the nation into social upheaval, Daniel Smiley and his sons had all they could do to keep the Mountain House secure, though the situation eased by 1920. Through prudent planning, careful budgeting, and personal physical strain, Daniel Smiley pulled Mohonk out of debt and kept a faithful clientele.

In spite of the difficulties inherent in wartime America, the planning of projects and new activities went forward. Radiators were finally installed throughout the House. With the coming of automobiles and trucks, a fireproof garage was built at Mountain Rest.

So committed were the Smileys and their guests to maintaining Mohonk's quality and its sense of purpose that despite the recession of 1919, Mohonk's fiftieth anniversary was celebrated by plans to erect a memorial tower to Albert Smiley. The tower was also to provide the New York State Conservation Department with a forest fire observation facility.

The years of World War I and those that followed brought about startling social changes in America. As a creation of a nineteenth-century ethos, Mohonk faced the challenge of survival. In its formative years it became a resort for people of reputation, means, and philanthropic influence. Its appointments were the most modern available at the time.

The clientele read as from a chapter on American business and social history, ranging from John Arbuckle, the coffee merchant, to John D. Rockefeller, the oil magnate, and from Mrs. Ulysses S. Grant to Helen M. Gould. Edward Everett Hale came to Mohonk to write in peace and John Burroughs came to savor and interpret the wonders of nature.

The problems posed by the post-war era might well have written Mohonk's last chapter, as happened to other resorts of an era now irrevocably lost. By clinging to a brilliant past and failing to adapt to an uncertain future they had lost their appeal and their survival. The prudent planning of Daniel Smiley and the unified efforts of his family created an atmosphere where Mohonk used its past as a basis for attraction and not reflection of past history. New approaches

(Opposite) The Mohonk House with its stone towers is reminiscent of a medieval castle when viewed from Eagle Cliff.

Mohonk

were designed for the Mohonk experience where guests could be challenged and stimulated to use all their faculties in helping discover the new needs of society and in the search for timeless values through contact with nature.

Opposite:
(Top left) Ceremony at the laying of the cornerstone for the Albert K. Smiley Memorial Tower on the point of Sky Top.

(Bottom left) Mohonk employed an artist to create a special cover for the 1920 advertising booklet. The original painting hangs in one of the hallways.

(Right) One of the regular participants in the Mohonk conferences was Edward Everett Hale, well known for his eloquence.

(This page) Stone Building, Parlor Wing, and East Porte-cochere from Pine Bluff.

Mohonk At Fifty

"In a very real sense we do not look upon ourselves as irresponsible owners but as trustees or stewards . . . ."
Daniel Smiley, Mohonk's 50th Anniversary exercises,
June 1, 1920

The construction of the Memorial Tower at Sky Top and the subsequent dedication exercises seemed a reaffirmation of Mohonk's purpose, its commitment to a quality resort experience as well as to the social goals maintained by the Smiley family. Daniel Smiley, with a propensity for organization and a management team including sons Albert and Francis served Mohonk well during the decade of the 1920's.

Reviewing briefly Daniel's role in the operation of Mohonk permits a better understanding of the atmosphere that Bert and Francis enjoyed as youths for empirical training in hotel management. It was indeed a baptism by experience. In 1881 Daniel had begun to take an active role in the management of the property. The entire House, save the section built in 1879 before his arrival, had been planned by him. Nearly all the roads came under his "engineering eye" and the development of forestry and the extensive Mohonk farm operation were his. Not trained as an engineer, Daniel, through acquired knowledge, supervised the planning of the civil, electrical, and mechanical engineering projects demanded by Mohonk's growth.

Just as Daniel had done for them, Francis and Bert began to train their children in the varied facets of the Mohonk business from the ground up. A typical set of experiences is expressed by Keith Smiley about the work that he and his brother Dan undertook:

> . . . the first job was painting signs; another activity we did through the same years was an unusual type of job and rather fascinating to us . . . somewhat like a treasure hunt. We were assigned periodically to comb the immediate area around the Mountain House for any sort of receptacle that might be a place where stagnant water could collect and breed mosquitoes, because before the days of all the sprays this was a practical way of getting rid of mosquito-breeding possibilities that might bother the guests. Also, we had traps for flies around the kitchen and dining rooms. Things of this sort were all special assignments.

Daniel was quite conscious of the strain of operating an efficient and gracious hotel, even though many of his guests were never aware of the problems he encountered. To keep a balance in life, he devoted much time to landscape gardening and the development of a subtle blend between natural scenery and the need to serve recreational purposes. As a result of these interests, he assembled an extensive and rare library on landscape gardening, forestry, and related subjects. This splendid collection guided the visual beauties of Mohonk which many visitors and guests credited to nature alone. The familiar figure of Daniel Smiley astride "Sunshine," his vigorous and handsome Kentucky-trained horse with natural "white socks," became a welcome sight to guests during the 1920's, as he rode about the grounds on tours of inspection.

Effie Smiley, complementing her husband's interests, took over supervision of the flower gardens

(Opposite) A carriage excursion is a good way to develop a full appreciation for Mohonk's varied scenery.

and the cultivated grounds around the Mountain House. As mistress of Mohonk, she served as the gracious hostess of numerous conferences and meetings and extended the kind word or helpful suggestion to guests. Her greatest love, however, was in plants and in providing a home life which, her husband noted, possessed rewards of "intangible influence and unheralded accomplishments." She, too, was a familiar figure driving her faithful horse, Kerney, about the Mohonk property with Borghild Fossum, her assistant and companion.

The Albert K. Smiley Memorial Tower, constructed from Shawangunk grit, quarried at its base in 1921, was completed in 1923 and dedicated on August 30. Allen and Collens, architects from Boston known for their Gothic revival buildings, conceived the plans for the now familiar landmark. Nearly one hundred guests contributed funds for the tower's construction. On the most exposed corner a turret specially designed for forest fire watches came into use and a watchman remained there until the early 1970's, when modern surveillance equipment replaced manpower. From the tower's observation roof, six states may be seen on a clear day—New York, Connecticut, Massachusetts, New Jersey, Pennsylvania, and Vermont.

The quarry left at the base of the tower became a reservoir, holding almost a million and a quarter gallons of water in reserve for additional fire protection by way of a 12-inch main extending to the House three hundred feet below. Appropriately, Bert Smiley oversaw the construction and coordinated the contribution efforts, a tower to honor the memory of his uncle, Albert K. Smiley, the founder of Mohonk.

Meanwhile, the automobile of the twentieth century remained something of an anathema to Daniel Smiley. While Mohonk's arriving guests were met in New Paltz by a Mohonk carriage until the early 1900's, after World War I the automobile began to replace the slower-paced horse-drawn vehicles. That the interests of time may have been well-served did not for Daniel Smiley make up for the gentle clomping of horses' hooves upon the winding shale-covered roads. The carriage possessed a graciousness and rhythm all its own and was to be replaced by the sputtering, gravel-gnashing auto, whose only purpose in life seemed to be speed and quick access. Daniel banned automobiles from the property. He wrote reprovingly in 1929:

> *Automobiles are kept out because they do not contribute to quiet and restfulness. To banish from this mountain noise and dirt and disorderliness, to keep the atmosphere sweet and clear, has been, and is, a primary aim requiring vigilance and labor and expense beyond belief. For this reason, at a great additional expense, hard instead of soft coal is burned at the power house. While the presence of automobiles would offend in these particulars, a great change has taken place also during the past ten years in the sentiments of those who use cars elsewhere and even make the journey here in them. The overwhelming consensus among guests has come to be that these are disturbers of quiet, however useful elsewhere, and should continue to be banished from this reservation. With minor and obvious exceptions, it is the well-known policy here to ascertain what guests desire and then give it to them. It is perfectly clear that for the present time the great majority of guests do not wish automobiles coming up to the door, while they do almost unanimously desire roads for horseback riding and walking to be free from sudden terror at every sharp turn around projecting bluffs.*

Later in the 1930's, after Daniel's death and the onset of the Depression, a modified decision was made: guests' automobiles were permitted to traverse Mohonk's roads, but a pilot from the Mountain House had to do the driving. In the 1950's the policy was changed to allow private-party cars to be driven by their owners. Even now, speed limits are 10 to 20 miles per hour and

signs admonish: "Slowly and Quietly, Please." Mohonk drivers are ordered to bring guests into the property slowly, so that time is allowed for unwinding and becoming mentally prepared for the Mohonk experience. Such a policy also helps to protect the many walkers and horseback riders.

Because of the automobile and the new mobility which it heralded, in 1925 Daniel Smiley and his sons constructed Lenape Lane in connection with an old stage road. This became the approach for cars through the Memorial Gateway up to Mountain Rest, the entrance point to the Mohonk House and grounds.

Run by J. Irving Goddard from 1891 to 1907, Mountain Rest was originally a boarding house begun by the Drew family. Guests at Mountain Rest could take advantage of the Mountain House programs and activities but stay in these less expensive quarters. Following its destruction by fire in 1907, the Mountain Rest business again appeared in the late teens as a bungalow colony and teahouse run by Hugh and Hester Smiley. Following the Hugh Smileys' departure from Mohonk, Irving Goddard came back to operate the Mountain Rest House and Cottages.

The 1920's saw another innovation by the Smileys. Mabel Craven Smiley wished to continue the family's concern for education. The distance to schools in nearby New Paltz became formidable in the winter for her children, Daniel, Keith, and Anna as well as for other mountain children. In 1920 Mabel became founder and owner of the Mohonk School. It was a private school for boys located on the Mohonk property in the Mountain House. The House, closed in the winter,

(Opposite top) Daniel Smiley and Sunshine, his favorite horse.

(Opposite bottom) This Mountain Rest House was opened in 1921. It provided less elaborate accommodations than those at the main House, and operated in conjunction with the cottage colony.

(Above) A Smiley family group photographed during Mohonk's Fiftieth Anniversary.

provided a means of using the facilities without inconveniencing the guests. During the Depression when the winter business was inaugurated to help keep the younger Smileys busy and augment Mohonk's income, the school changed to a junior school format rather than exclusively college preparatory, and the Smiley Brothers took over ownership. Beginning in 1958, Mr. and Mrs. E.M. Lafferty, former principals at Mohonk, continued the venture as a separate entity from Mohonk. The Mohonk School was moved to the Cragsmoor Inn and later again moved, to a location near Wallkill, New York.

During these years and to a large extent for the two following decades, self-sufficiency was one of the hallmarks of the Mohonk operation. Daniel and Effie had worked closely with Bert and Mabel and with Francis and Rachel. They had the opportunity of watching their grandchildren grow up in the Mohonk environment.

A group of Mohonk farms provided the Mountain House with fresh milk, some fresh vegetables and meats. Refuse from the hotel kitchen was fed to the pigs; the pig farm produced pork. Animal fats, salvaged in the kitchen, were used to manufacture a yellow soap which in turn was used in the kitchen and laundry. The operation of the farms by 1930 saw nearly forty men employed, working with twenty horses and two tractors. Nearly 1,000 acres of Mohonk land were cultivated or in pasture. Francis Smiley took special interest in the dairy herds and the pig farm, and in keeping the extensive records on both.

Until 1958 Mohonk also produced its own electrical and heating power, using expensive hard coal which burned cleaner for energy efficiency and for low pollution. Wood served as the principal fuel used in the power plant during the Depression of the 1930's and during World War II. Guests of long standing and those familiar with the Smiley management of Mohonk view the recent national concern for ecology with some irony, since for so long have such life relationships been studied and practiced by the stewards of Mohonk.

Daniel Smiley's sense of humor and ability to suffer lightly many minor but irritating problems in managing Mohonk remind one of his fine qualities. The no-pet rule has been thrashed about over the years by management and guests alike. In 1925 Daniel wrote an engaging account laced with humor by reaffirming why pets were not, and still are not, allowed at Mohonk:

> *During fifty years at one time or another attempts have been made to keep about every kind of pet animal, bird and reptile, from the bear to white mice. All have proved to be undesirable and wholly incompatible with the comfort and safety of guests. They have accordingly been summarily banished, including cats and dogs of all sizes and lineage. Even crow or fox in cages excite commiseration and protest from the tender-hearted. Thus the keeping of some in confinement excites pity to an uncomfortable degree; others have proved intolerable on account of noise; others, like dogs and cats, are regarded with fear by an astonishingly large number of people; others have unexpectedly proved to be directly or indirectly dangerous,—such as the flight of our gorgeous pet peacocks, Jupiter and Juno, frightening horses and causing runaways. Even the very few remaining wild creatures which are disposed to be friendly are not wholly without offence. Not all enjoy the cunning chipmunk in his visits to rooms in search of nuts and sweetmeats. Even the harmless woodchuck, 'Betsy,' with her young family grazing on the western lawn has been avoided with fear by not a few, to whom she appears as a wild beast of fearful dimensions and fierceness. Dogs are dogs, whether big or little, aristocratic or plebeian, and are not allowed in the House, nor on the property except on leash. Experience has made this question not open to argument. For visitors to meet any kind of welcome the dog must be left behind. Other animal or bird or reptile pets are repulsed with the same hard-hearted insistence. We love peace and are not knowingly inviting discord and strife, unseemly words and unkind thoughts among Mohonk guests. To many people, as to all the Mohonk family, pets of many kinds are delightful at home, but a decent respect for the feelings of others bars them from this place.*

Suddenly, late in October of 1929 Daniel Smiley suffered a stroke and for ten weeks underwent a series of medical treatments. As late as January 1930 he prepared to go west with Effie to spend the winter recuperating in Redlands, California, but he took a turn for the worse in February. Surrounded by his family on the estate he had helped to build, expand, and make famous for forty-eight years, Daniel died on February 14, 1930. Simple funeral services were conducted the following Monday at the Mountain House by the Reverend Mr. Hageman, widely known as a pastor of the Dutch Reformed Church. At noon a brief service was held in the Quaker Meeting House in Poughkeepsie, with Samuel Eliot, a close friend of Daniel's, presiding. Daniel's finest eulogy—the most accurate testament to his life's work—came from the *New York Times*, whose obituary stated his occupation as simply, but significantly, "humanitarian."

(Opposite, top left) The third in the series of towers on Sky Top is the Albert K. Smiley Memorial, constructed of conglomerate rock. The quarry was lined and became a reflecting pool as well as a reservoir.

(Opposite, top right) Until 1965 when mechanical refrigeration took over, natural ice was harvested from the lake each winter.

(Opposite, bottom) A wooden observation tower was erected on Sky Top in 1872. It was the first of three successive towers at this location.

(Above) In the 1920's, the students of The Mohonk School began to keep a rink cleared for ice hockey.

Transition And A Depression

"We remember a little more clearly those painful 'budget-slashing'
years of the 1930 Depression, when men were happy to chop wood
for board and one dollar per day."
                    A. Keith Smiley, Story of Mohonk

Depression. Only those who went through the Great Depression of the 1930's can internalize the outward signs of want—breadlines, staggering unemployment, food shortage, bank failures. Only those in the ferment of that economic tumult can testify to the accompanying spiritual depression of anxiety, uncertainty, and fear.

It was during the national economic crisis that Bert and Francis inherited the Mohonk operation from Daniel. Fortunately, their own training and perspicacity brought new talents and energy to face a multiplicity of problems. Not long after the beginning of the Depression, the three children of Bert and Mabel began to assist in the business. Their daughter, Anna C. Smiley, helped with the guest entertainment, the weekly *Bulletin,* and purchasing. In 1941 she married Donald E. Richardson, who was Headmaster of the Mohonk School from the late 1930's until soon after the beginning of the Second World War, when they moved away to engage in other activities.

Heretofore the story of Mohonk reflected the challenges of creation, identity, acceptance, and harnessing the thrust of success in philanthropic directions. In 1930 new times were at hand, and many of the loyal and influential guests of the first generation had passed from the scene, along with Mohonk's founders. The challenge now lay in keeping the patronage of the "regulars," holding on to faithful employees, and stabilizing Mohonk's expenses while attracting additional guests. When money is more readily available, it is less arduous to manage a business. Not that Albert or Daniel had put in less effort nor that their challenges were less formidable, but the 1930's presented harsh realities that greatly altered Mohonk's serenity. It was a sheer, dogged determination "to keep going" that impelled Bert and Francis Smiley to push and labor in Mohonk's behalf. Survival was the word; survival in a world gone mad politically, disjointed economically, and impoverished in spirit. A resort hotel was far down the list of pressing national concerns.

In 1933, partially in response to economic exigencies but also due to guest inquiries, Francis and Bert Smiley decided to experiment with a partial winter opening. For sixty-two years the winter months had been set aside for repair, cleaning, and renovation. Mohonk employees annually scattered for a warmer winter climate and employment in Florida, Arizona, or California. Indeed, the senior Smileys, A.K. and Eliza, rarely remained at Mohonk after the first of November, nor returned much before May first.

The decision to open part of the House for winter guests necessitated the development of winter sports and activities: sledding, ice skating on the lake, sleigh rides, and indoor amusement. Much later skiing would augment the winter programming, with ski-touring growing fast in recent years.

(Opposite) Mohonk in winter garb.

(Above) Mohonk has retained an unusual collection of horse-drawn vehicles in its Barn Museum; some of the old-fashioned sleighs and carriages are still used.

(Above right) The Grove and Central sections of the Mountain House (right) remain open in winter. Skating is conveniently available nearby.

The contrast of a present-day winter season with the long-standing winter routine is seen in this description of winter duties compiled by Daniel Smiley, shortly before his death:

> When the House closes for guests in the autumn, immediate preparation for the next season begins. For three months in autumn and spring the housekeeper has a company . . . . men and women taking up, cleaning and relaying carpets, papering, painting, varnishing and renovating rooms. The man in charge of sanitation, while busy every day in the year, has his inning at all places then unoccupied. This is an important office, waging unremitting war on the whole race of undesirable germ-producing citizens, out-of-doors and within, ranging in size all the way up from the minute organism scarcely visible under a microscope, to rats and weasels and the night-prowling dog in guilty quest of garbage and trouble generally. A force of plumbers, too, is busy all winter, and carpenters making repairs outside and in. There are ten to twenty painters on wagons and automobiles, which are also overhauled and repairs made. Light driving horses are put in box stalls and have yards for exercise. A part of the 2500-ton coal supply is drawn up the mountain. The aim is to cut and draw to the power house two thousand cords of wood each winter.
>
> The slate-crushing plant and the Shawangunk grit plant are also operated to provide a supply of surfacing material for roads, and many miles of our drives and paths re each year covered with these materials. The cutting of wood and timber is done on scientific private estate and forestry lines with a view to encouraging laurel, dogwood, azalea,

*rhododendron, and other flowering plants, as well as trees having beautiful autumn
foliage; and there is also cutting away trees to open distant views. In the winter the
greenhouses and thousands of bedding plants require attention . . . There is in autumn
the fertilizing of flower beds and lawns and covering tender plants with leaves and pine
boughs, and in the spring the care of hotbeds and sowing of flower seed and the putting
out of thousands of annuals, and planting trees in cultivated ground and woods . . .
Keeping open roads after each snowstorm, and shovelling enormous drifts from roofs
of buildings all continue. Provisions and coal and a vast variety of supplies must be
drawn by horses when snow is too deep for auto truck, and ice gathered from the lake
. . . Watchmen go their rounds indoors and out. The laundry is operated. Hickory and
rock oak, too, must be drawn to the big woodshed and sawed by power and split by
hand and piled to season and be ready for the cheerful open fires.*

With the help of Mabel's and Bert's sons, Daniel and Keith, the 1930's saw a host of improvements
and innovation at Mohonk. The Mountain House for the most part was equipped with automatic
sprinklers for fire protection. The first rock climbing took place on the Trapps. Another activity
begun during this period was the Mohonk Trail Riders, originated by Edward B. Jones, the
House manager. The first trip began in October 1932, and the fee charged was $35 for three days.
Fifty miles were ridden in two days along mountain trails. Those who completed the fifty-mile
trek were awarded a horse collar. The calamity of World War II ended the Mohonk Trail Riders,
who made their last trip in 1942. The Shongum Outing Club took its first walk in 1933 in
September. The members traversed many of the carriage roads and trails in rugged mountain
country. These outings were usually three days in duration and have continued in modified form
to the present time under the name "Hikers Holiday."

Out of economic adversities came still other innovations and a subtle, distinct change in
Mohonk's strategy. Where conferences and philanthropic outreach had been predominant prior
to the First World War, a new era was now at hand. The energies of the family were being used to
safeguard Mohonk's tradition and its very existence. This called for the utilization of Mohonk's
resources not only on behalf of guests but also in a variety of other activities. The period between
1930 and 1960 saw increased concentration on streamlining the farms and sale of products of the
land, and more intensive efforts to maintain the expected services to guests with a smaller staff.
More and more college students and non-professional employees became part of Mohonk's
fabric of service.

Certainly, without the backing of faithful and sympathetic employees, Mohonk's story would be
far different and less fruitful. "The success of this enterprise depends on employees no less than
on its owner," Daniel Smiley had observed. Many of the Mohonk employees came to the
Mountain House in their teens or early twenties and left in their sixties. At Mohonk it was
nothing out of the ordinary to have employees recognized for fifteen to twenty years of service
and others up to twenty-five or thirty years. A few piled up even more years. Earl Stokes, a great-
grandson of John Stokes from whom Albert and Alfred Smiley bought Mohonk in 1869, after
serving many years in various farm jobs, ended his career as head farmer. As of this writing, he
works at the Mohonk Barn Museum.

In a number of cases three generations of the same family have worked at Mohonk. In an
operation like the Mountain House, the contact between employee and guest frequently becomes
an association eagerly looked forward to as the season begins. Conversely, employees at Mohonk,
and needless to say the Smileys themselves, suffer well the over-enthusiastic proprietary nature of

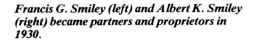

*Francis G. Smiley (left) and Albert K. Smiley
(right) became partners and proprietors in
1930.*

some guests. The affinity for Mohonk is such among many of the regulars that the Smileys must patiently listen to management suggestions, commentary about the food, criticism of a wall color or opinions about Mohonk in days gone by. Occasionally the guest who is a "perennial commentator" must be set into line. Amusing reading may be found in the old correspondence files of past managers who sought to pour oil on troubled waters and to calm a tempest in a teapot. " A soft voice turneth away wrath," is the unwritten rule among Mohonk's employees.

The Smileys' concern for employees is evidenced throughout. The balcony of the present parlor was installed so that employees might enjoy the rich and varied musical, cultural, and lecture programs of the House. This assured that seats for the guests in the parlor would not be taken up by the employees, yet all had access to the programs.

These were very active years for Bert Smiley's wife, Mabel Craven Smiley. For a long period she had lent her guidance in matters of housekeeping and employee relations. During her more than sixty years of continuous residence at Mohonk, the welfare of employees was one of her special concerns. She was interested in their recreational needs and helped arrange for parties and library facilities. She also served as unofficial but much appreciated counselor for both personal and business problems. Mabel Smiley died in 1972, but appreciation of her kindly spirit continues in the memory of many guests and employees.

The presence of employees who live nearby leads to an efficient use of part-time workers and flexibility in the use of many talents exercised by Mohonk's staff. The employee at Mohonk is an integral part of an operation which for well over a hundred years has sought to create a world of "law and not accident," as Daniel Smiley referred to it.

Early in the 1900's a group of Mohonk employees decided to formalize an employees' group. From the minute book of the "Mohonkers" comes the following explanation:

> *For many years, through the hospitality of Loren R. Johnston, a number of employees of Mohonk Mountain House have been privileged to attend, each autumn, an annual banquet at Picnic Lodge. These events have been the most attractive feature of the season and have been greatly enjoyed by all. In 1902 it was decided that these meetings should be formally organized so as to become a permanent feature of Mohonk life.*

Ben Matteson, executive vice president, wrote an account of the "Mohonkers" in an August 1976 Bulletin. It not only provides the historic setting for this employees' group but also the gratitude of management for the many faithful and loyal people who were or are employed at Mohonk:

> *Although the Society (Mohonkers) was somewhat secret in nature and its members were sworn to keep the initiation ceremony from public knowledge, meetings were attended by invited non-members and the society's purpose was, obviously, good fellowship. Meetings were held once a year in October and started rather late—about 11:00 p.m.—extending well into the morning of the next day. The first formal initiation ceremony was held at the fourth annual meeting, October 11, 1905. Following this, the members enjoyed the traditional banquet of oyster stew, salad, dessert and coffee, followed by cigars. A series of formal toasts were made—with coffee— to "Our Organization," "Our Association," "Our Profession," "Our Friends," and "Our Banquet." All present were called upon to respond with appropriate remarks. Since there were then 20 members present, this took until 4:10 a.m. Not all of the Mohonkers' meetings were as long and many undertook serious discussion. The meetings continued each year until 1932, after which the meetings ended as the Depression gripped Mohonk and the country. How many successful Mohonkers got their start here and how much Mohonk owes to this continued association with previous employees is hard to calculate . . . we frequently communicate with previous employees. Mohonk is a powerful source of brotherhood and inspiration.*

The Mohonk employees over the years formed a number of group activities including baseball teams, variety shows, and even a band. The Smileys' appreciation for employee morale has been demonstrated over and over again in the more than 100 years of their ownership of Mohonk. In 1907 Picnic Lodge was built with the express goal of having a place for employees to congregate socially, as well as partake in refreshments and buy sundries. In 1978, after a period of inactivity, Picnic Lodge once again was renovated for employee use, as well as being a center for day visitors. One of the happy circumstances enjoyed by employees is the continuing policy of encouraging activities for sociability.

Opposite:
(Top) The Mohonk Trail Riders, a group organized by Edward B. Jones of the House staff, met twice a year for two full days of riding.

(Middle) Economies resulting from the Depression led to large-scale cutting of wood in the Mohonk forests to produce fuel for the power plant.

(Bottom) Mabel Craven Smiley, whose father was one of the Old Boys of Mohonk, had been a guest with her family for a number of years before marrying into the Smiley family.

(Top right) The first organized Hikers week-end took place in 1933. It was then known as the Shongum Outing Club, and later became Hikers Holiday covering a full week in May.

Above:
Rachel Orcutt Smiley, with her husband, Francis, at the choralcelo, a gift of Conference attenders. Over the years many guests have appreciated Rachel's music on the choralcelo and its successor, the Allen organ.

Chapter Thirteen
A New Business Order

"... Her serenity of outlook undergirded the efforts of other
members of the family, as they struggled successively with ...
Depression, world war, rationing, and inflation."
Effie Smiley as described by grandson, A. Keith Smiley, 1953

With the death of Effie Smiley, Daniel's wife, on May 14, 1951, a chapter in Mohonk's history closed. All who knew her, whether guest, employee, or family, came away impressed with her kindly spirit, gentle manner, and strong supportive qualities. From 1880 to 1950, Effie beheld the growth of Mohonk as a resort and the expansion of its influence. She knew presidents and foreign ministers, famous artists, and imposing merchants. Yet her modest and winning ways treated all alike, whether employee, guest, or conference delegate. During the Depression years and World War II when all America saw old ways and many traditions knocked into a "cocked hat," Effie Smiley provided a personal continuity while her family sought to change, to modify, to face expenses while maintaining the quality and the core of Mohonk's purposes and guest services. Effie had seen the coming of electric lights and automobiles, massive social upheavals and the birth of the nuclear age brought upon the world. She also saw Mohonk—its outlook in seeking harmony between people and between people and nature—still remain "Mohonk."

In anticipation of the day when leadership would change in the business, Bert and Francis began to plan for a transition in Mohonk's structure. The 1930 partnership between Albert and Francis became extended in 1953 to include Bert's sons, Daniel and Keith (A.K.S., Jr.) and Francis' son, Gerow. This not only allowed incorporation of the land which would make a more manageable transfer of property to succeeding generations but also updated the business for the new round of inheritance and business taxes.

The Lake Mohonk Corporation was formed to own the property. The five partners continued to lease the land and operate the resort. Bert and Francis saw to the operations and comfort of guests. Bert also advised on finance and the park department. Francis concentrated on accounting, engineering, and grounds. Dan served as controller and saw to engineering, as well as to purchasing building and grounds materials. Keith gave attention to the "front of the house," advertising, and the *Mohonk Bulletin,* while Gerow applied his energies to personnel and farm operations.

Mohonk's owners and their wives often wore various "hats" when it came to duties about the house and grounds. This is still true today. Nature walks had to be led and lectures given on flora and fauna as well as Mohonk history. Mabel Smiley began arranging for the weekly resident clergymen, while Rachel secured the musicians for the parlor musicals.

The 1950's ushered in a host of improvements at Mohonk including the first electric power supplied by the Central Hudson Gas & Electric Corporation rather than by the Mohonk power plant. The first alternating current at the House itself came in 1958, also provided by Central Hudson. Use of Mohonk lands was facilitated through such devices as a camping permit system.

(Opposite) Physical features of the swimming area, bathing apparel, and cultural patterns have all undergone marked changes since the days when parasols were more important than sun floats.

(Above) The Mohonk show garden, planted every year with many varieties of annuals.

(Above right) When this scene was typical of "Bathing in Mohonk Lake," the flat-bottomed boats of earlier days had been replaced by St. Lawrence skiffs or rowboats.

(Right) The Putting Green, with its unusually fine turf, is the result of careful nurture over many years.

A variety of organizations utilized Mohonk's facilities and ambience for important meetings. Over 100 different YMCA conferences alone had met over the years at Mohonk. Other groups included the Layman's Foreign Mission Inquiry; New York State Library Association; the Conference on Science, Philosophy and Religion; American Telephone and Telegraph Company executives; an institute on cancer research; an assortment of local and regional agencies; and a number of industry workshops and training sessions. In 1956 the Board of Foreign Missions of the Presbyterian Church held an important meeting at Mohonk for the purpose of drafting a new plan of action.

During this period the Smileys realized that changing times necessitated a new approach toward conferences. It came to be realized that groups and organizations could be assisted to glean the best from the setting and the environment at Mohonk while running their own meetings. Mohonk's contribution to group deliberations would take a new form. Important conferences for diplomats from the United Nations were and are convened at Mohonk. These meetings are jointly sponsored by The Mohonk Trust and the American Friends Service Committee. Programs such as these are a continuing demonstration of the Smileys' abiding concern for international understanding. The Mohonk Trust, about which more will be said, is a separate and distinct organization from the Mountain House business.

The seeds of new structures were sown during the so-called quiet fifties. When the social upheavals of the 1960's fell upon the land, it would not be an easy time for Mohonk, but thanks to a penchant for grappling with change, it was a fruitful time.

(Above) The double-story summerhouse at the Bathing Beach, reflected in the waters of the lake. After these rustic structures were located on the projecting boulders near the shore, the area was called Swiss Lake Village.

(Opposite) Cross-country skiers breaking trail across Mohonk Lake.

(Above left) Activities staff and helpers prepare griddle cakes and sausage for a breakfast cookout at Open Camp by the lake.

(Above right) The building now known as the Council House was built in 1876 and is the oldest structure still standing in the immediate vicinity of the lake. It was used as a bowling alley until 1960 when it was changed into a conference center to help fill a growing need.

Recognition

"Mohonk has always been dedicated to the spiritual and physical
refreshment of all who need it, and can appreciate it."
Mohonk Bulletin, *September 1962*

Francis G. Smiley died peacefully on July 14, 1962. His death was unexpected and filled the hearts of guests and employees alike with much sadness. In the *Mohonk Bulletin* a special memorial was printed:

> *Some people's lives are like a pebble dropped in the ocean.*
>
> *Such was the life of Francis Gerow Smiley. Lived in one small spot with quiet integrity, intense loyalty, a devotion to duty which defies description, and a thoroughly delightful sense of humor, it has yet affected untold thousands of guests, who, through the years, have carried home with them the blessings of his gentle presence. For some, the memories will center on his kindly advice with their fishing problems; for others, it will be the spiritual benefits of his conduct of the daily Morning Prayer service which will remain.*
>
> *We are grateful for his years of service, and the warmth of his life, which will linger on with that of his father and uncle, to become an integral part of the "spirit of Mohonk."*

In 1964 Mohonk friends, in gratitude for the life and work of Francis Smiley, contributed in his memory a new Allen organ for the Parlor. There the sounds of music serve as a reminder of the service and dedication that Francis gave to Mohonk and his role in assuring its survival.

Only two years later, Mohonk's friends would again be saddened by the news of Albert "Bert" Smiley's death on November 9, 1964. For over fifty years Bert Smiley, like his brother Francis, had wrestled with the dual challenge of keeping a family business running and seeking a balance between existence and higher motives behind Mohonk's purpose. Excerpts from his correspondence reveal that he and his relatives sought always to follow Daniel's dictum that "guests should never see the wheels turning."

For those who might have the impression that owning Mohonk was, or is, all sweetness and joy, an enclave apart from life's grueling realities, they need only peruse Bert's correspondence files to correct such misimpressions. The following excerpt from a letter to his father strikes a responsive chord in those people today who feel overwhelmed by the mountain of paper:

> *There is much food for thought in this letter of thine, as in many others, but so far, I have not had much time to do the necessary thinking. Although I am making a real effort to carry out the arrangement of my work, according to thy suggestions, I am afraid I am not making much progress, and at times I am considerably discouraged in my inability to delegate very much of the work to others. In these times, at least, I think it is best to interview the employees myself; and besides that I really enjoy getting around the country a little, especially with the car, and it gets me away from the grind*

(Opposite) For over ninety years farming was a part of the Mohonk enterprise on the lower hillsides and bottomlands on both sides of the mountain. With the 1960's came a transition to leasing farm areas.

(Top left) Climbing up rustic ladders in the Great Crevice.

(Top right) Music has always been an integral part of life at Mohonk. In recent years it has burst into a new form with the annual Octoberfest of Chamber Music.

at the desk and the everlasting memorandums and reports that have grown so now that it is about one man's job to read them over and get them placed where they belong, let alone putting much time studying on them. If I had time to properly digest all the stuff it would be mighty pleasant and a great benefit to read them; but as it is, it seems to me just so much stuff every day to plow through and get rid of during the evening and between times.

Yet, through it all, the delights of having one's family amid such surroundings, the companionship of good friends, and the beauties of nature on the Mohonk property, enlivened and gave purpose to both Francis' and Bert Smiley's lives. In 1969 some of Mohonk's guests, who through the years were close to Bert, felt there should be some permanent memorial as a reminder of his love for and contributions to Mohonk. Remembering his interest in the outdoors, a committee, led by Warren L. Cruikshank, agreed with the Smiley family that a rose garden would be a suitable memorial.

This portion of the garden, with a seat built of cedar from trees grown on Mohonk soil and a plaque bearing Albert K. Smiley's name, was dedicated on July 8, 1969, as one feature of the 100th anniversary celebrations.

(Above left) On the Fourth of July the porches of the House become the spectators' gallery for the traditional water sports.

(Above right) In 1963 a new Allen Organ replaced the aging Choralcelo. It was given to Mohonk in memory of Francis Smiley by a large group of guests.

(Left) In 1969 the Albert K. Smiley Memorial Rose Garden was dedicated as part of Mohonk's Centennial program.

Chapter Fifteen
The 1960's

*"I like this room so much that I would be sorely tempted to put its
authentic period elegance more in formal order, but not at the risk
of destroying its air of easy survival and comfortable use from
past to present."*

Ada Louise Huxtable, writing of the Mohonk Parlor
in The New York Times.

The 1960's proved to be times of rapid change for the Smiley family and their operation of the
Lake Mohonk Mountain House. They also brought severe tests to Mohonk's inherent strengths
and necessitated important decisions. The discussions over transitional problems, as well as the
persistent challenge of how to keep the operation going and save the land, occasioned frank and
often lively exchanges. The deaths of Francis and Bert were followed closely by the decision of
Gerow Smiley not to remain active in the Mohonk business but rather to pursue his profession of
veterinary medicine in northern California.

The departure of some members of the family from the day-to-day management of the business
led to the necessity for reorganization. Questions of succession in ownership were resolved by a
new structure. Out of extensive legal, family, and personal discussions came Smiley Brothers, Inc.
organized in 1969. This group included A. Keith Smiley, Daniel Smiley, Gerow Smiley, and
Smiley Brothers Trust (a business trust set up to meet certain legal and tax requirements). The
latter group consisted of a board of trustees made up of Smiley family and non-family members.
Thus, continuity was provided in the event of the inactivity or death of the present stockholders
or if no new leadership emerged from among the younger members of the Smiley family.

The Board of Directors of Smiley Brothers, Inc. elected Benjamin H. Matteson to be the first
Executive Vice President of the new corporation, and at this writing he continues in that capacity,
with the responsibilities of general manager. Ben's wife is Rachel Smiley Matteson (daughter of
Francis and Rachel Smiley), whose contributions to Mohonk operations are described in
Chapter Eighteen. Ben had grown up in New Paltz, where his father taught at the State
University College; before coming to Mohonk most of his work was with the nearby branch of
IBM, as a mechanical engineer. He brought to his new position a familiarity with the area and an
awareness of Mohonk's philosophy.

The social upheavals of the 1960's provided observers of American life with a ringside seat before
conflicting values and ideologies. Pressures to throw out the old and bring in the new affected
every institution, and Mohonk was no exception. In a July 1967 article in the *Mohonk Bulletin,*
Dan Smiley's wife, Virginia, noted: "We don't *want* to make a chrome-shining avant-garde
replica of a modern resort hotel out of the old, comfortable, beloved House that we have." Yet
the Smileys were aware that new efforts in programming were going to be needed for many new
guests whose backgrounds were far different from the original clientele of the 1870's. Continuity,
however, remained an essential in guest perceptions of Mohonk. It meant, as the *Bulletin* observed,
that guests came to the Parlor "for talks on everything from folklore to flying saucers, for formal
concerts and community sings, for morning prayers and travel talks." "The library," it noted,
"one of the largest and most comprehensive available in a resort hotel, is in constant use . . . ."

*(Opposite) Mohonk maintains many miles of
roads and trails suitable for horseback riding.*

Our Snow is Old Fashioned

But let's face it, so are we. To us snow spells white landscapes and healthy appetites. (Yes, sir, you may have "seconds".) It's family fun time.

No modern machine-made snow for us. It wouldn't even know how to blanket a pine tree. Or put a white wig on Washington's profile. Or a toupee on bald rocks. That synthetic stuff's only for fancy ski resorts.

Our skiing and snowshoeing are for people who like the challenge of going up — and across — as well as down. Sledding too — you walk up. (It's your third helping, sir, but who's counting?)

Funny how many people pay a neighbor's kid to dig out their driveway. So they can come to Mohonk and help shovel off the skating rink! Sure it makes sense: If you're going to stimulate your appetite, do it where the food is good, and **you** don't have to prepare it. Like at Mohonk. (No, sir, I'm not counting. But it was your fourth, sir.)

We're open from December 26, 1962, to February 25, 1963. By all means bring the children. Our 7,500 acres of snow are waiting to be converted into snow-men, forts, tunnels, and butterflies. (You can't eat any more? What a pity! But you'll sleep well tonight!)

SMILEY BROTHERS

LAKE MOHONK MOUNTAIN HOUSE
Mohonk Lake, New Paltz, N.Y.

(Above) A direct-mail flyer, used in the 1960's, encouraged guests to see Mohonk in the winter.

(Above right) The bird fountain in a corner of the garden was presented to Mohonk by a guest.

(Right) Tour groups frequently come to see the flowers; garden walks and greenhouse tours are regularly scheduled during the summer season.

As Mohonk headed towards its 100th anniversary in 1969 the Smiley family in essence spent the latter 1960's asking themselves as well as the guests: "What do you want of us?" In a sense the query was a conundrum; guests want "sameness," yet the demands of time and circumstance force, or at least involve, change. Some guests clamor, "Don't change anything!" But horses no longer bring guests to the door in carriages; evening dresses for women and black ties for men on Friday evening are seen less often! Still, the spirit, the essence, of Mohonk survived the vagaries of the 1960's in much the same form as when Albert Smiley began his enterprise. As the *Mohonk Bulletin* reminded people:

> *We must remember that what we derive from any experience is directly related to what we bring to it. The degree of our enrichment hinges directly on the quality of our own spiritual baggage, and the degree of our involvement. Total involvement brings great rewards, emotionally and spiritually.*

> *The qualities which you bring to Mohonk determine what you shall get from your visit. We can entertain most guests at one time or another, in one way or another. But we want to do much more than that; we want to make your experience here a deeply meaningful and rewarding one. No matter how hard we work, the quality of your Mohonk experience depends not on the physical possessions that you bring, but what you carry in your heart.*

In a real sense one can say that Mohonk has not emphasized *change* but rather *enhancement*. Albert Smiley's beautiful dream of a resort to recreate mind, soul and body, and as a place where good causes and impulses would be well served, became a responsibility. We can never be sure whether the dream preceded the purchase of land at Mohonk or whether it lay inherent in Smiley's soul only awaiting the vehicle of expression. The dream did not fade during the succeeding generation, but circumstances surrounding two world wars made survival a major concern in this perpetual haven of beauty, peace and love. And behind all this was the raven-like refrain of the guests, "Don't let Mohonk change! Don't let Mohonk change!"

Mohonk Elevatoriana

Third floor, Sir? — I'm sorry, this is the Thursday trip to the fourth floor!

Two hand-operated hydraulic elevators served guests for over seventy years. Their deliberate mode of operation was turned into an asset in this promotional cartoon, through such phrases as "easy on the stomach."

(Opposite) Mohonk Lake has provided uncounted happy days for fishermen.

(Above) The Granary, which derives its name from earlier use as storage place for deer food, has been transformed into a service area for light meals during the summer.

Chapter Sixteen
The Mohonk Trust: An Innovation

*"In a sense, the two main objectives of The Mohonk Trust,
fostering peace among men and serving to spread the ecological
ethic, are really but the two sides of the same coin, the
enlightened participation in the life that man and his associate
species of plants and animals share."*
From a Mohonk Trust Educational Release
by Carl J. George

A number of interrelated factors were involved in the decision to establish The Mohonk Trust.

The initial exploration was motivated by a desire to see Mohonk continue to serve its traditional roles in a changing world. Fundamental was the desire to continue the resort operation and, simultaneously, to maintain the Smiley family's role of actively encouraging a better life for human beings and peaceable relations among them. It was hoped that this combination of goals might be accomplished within the context of the interdependence of all life on our planet— humans, animals, trees, plants, the forces of nature.

As this aim was beginning to be formulated more clearly, a serendipitous event occurred. A close friend and frequent guest discussed with members of the family possible ways of keeping these concerns alive and integrating them with the total Mohonk enterprise. His suggestion resulted in harnessing the energies of a number of Mohonk friends who would help build the objectives into an organization.

The initial exploration became linked with an exciting compatible objective, namely, to put into practice and test new concepts of land stewardship. Use of the land would be encouraged for purposes of education, scientific study, inspiration, and recreation.

The Mohonk Trust was founded in 1963. The basic forces resulting in its birth were the intense desire to reinforce long-standing social concerns and a motivation to demonstrate that a valuable acreage of open space can be maintained for purposes of public benefit through a combination of contributions and fees collected from visitors. Hence the Trust, by the terms of its agreement, is committed to two interrelated objectives: the improvement of human understanding and cooperation on a world basis, and fostering the concept that humans are indeed a part of the total web of life on planet Earth. The Trust is a non-profit organization and is entirely separate, legally and financially, from the corporation which operates the Mohonk Mountain House.

The first land acquisition by the Trust consisted of property over a mile from the resort itself. Environmental concerns related to the stewardship of Trust lands have rapidly expanded since 1963. Studies involving Mohonk flora and fauna are being carried on. Trust researchers put to use the extensive weather records (kept by the Mohonk House, starting in 1896) along with many years of botanical and zoological observations made by members of the Smiley family and others. However, the Trust's research is not an end in itself. Its studies have proved to be invaluable as sources of information for three areas of public benefit, namely: 1) education and interpretation; 2) stewardship of the Trust's preserve; and 3) cooperation with researchers from other institutions, both public and private.

The educational programs of the Trust have been evolving as experience was gained and opportunities arose. School and college classes, as well as adult groups, regularly profit from the

*(Opposite) A Trust-sponsored school group
exploring Bonticou Crag.*

(Above) Rock climbing is one of the most popular activities on Trust land.

(Above right) The Trust has cooperated in the effort of Cornell University to re-establish nesting sites of the peregrine falcon along the Shawangunk escarpment. These boxes are for the protection of the young birds.

unique nature trails and study sites on Trust land. Independent studies have been carried out by many students.

By the late 1970's the Trust land was host to some 30,000 visitors each year. This involved activities that are appropriate to the natural landscape, such as hiking, cross country skiing, nature study, photography, camping, hunting, horseback riding, and rock climbing. In combination or individually, such enjoyment of the natural benefits of the land has contributed to "the mental and moral improvement of men, women, and children."

Up to February 1980, 5,280 acres of wild land have been acquired by purchase and gift. The majority of this was from holdings of the Smiley family. However, the resort still owns about 2,200 acres surrounding the hotel.

The effort to stimulate new approaches to real estate tax practices has not been easy for the Trust. A new venture of this kind was exposed to many misunderstandings by neighbors and the general public. One example of these difficulties should help to round out this aspect of Mohonk history. In 1974 the township of Gardiner, in which the Trust holds considerable acreage, challenged the tax-exempt status of the Trust as related to provisions of the New York State real estate tax laws. The legal proceedings which followed were carried on over nearly five years. Decisions of the lower courts denied the Trust's tax-exempt status. In 1979 an appeal to the highest court of the state resulted in the reversal of those decisions. The ruling confirmed the Trust's exempt status, and included the purposes of the Trust, its organizational structure, and the nature of its activities. In the meantime, open-space covenants had been entered into with the four townships where the Trust owns large amounts of land. These recognized the reduced value of the land due to restrictions on development, yet enabled the towns to receive revenues commensurate with the cost of the public services required.

Activities promoting understanding between persons have also expanded. They started in 1963 with the sponsorship of a Thanksgiving-time international student consultation. Through these gatherings an opportunity was provided for students to evaluate their experience in the United States and to be assisted in the development of skills and perspectives for an effective transition from their studies in the United States to useful careers and satisfying lives in their home countries. Also, in more recent years, by co-hosting International Peace Academy seminars and discussions for United Nations diplomats, the Trust continues the Smiley family interest and commitment toward seeking peaceful solutions to world problems.

The trustees meet regularly to hear reports from Trust committees and personnel regarding international and educational activities and in regard to the ongoing work of preserving, studying, and enhancing the resources of Trust lands. At present (1980), the activities are burgeoning: research includes more than seventy projects involving institutions and individuals; programs arranged for school and college students require half of the Trust naturalist's effort; interpretation of nature comes through guided public walks; and a newsletter and other special publications reach a wide readership.

While the mechanism in achieving the founders' goals has had to adjust to new demands and a changing world, the philosophy behind Albert K. Smiley's hope is very much a part of Mohonk:

> *I trust that many generations . . . will . . . find on the height not only a well-ordered hostelry, but more—a home where warmest greeting will be extended and friendships cultivated; still more, that eminent men shall meet here to discuss great national and international questions that pertain to the betterment of the world; and above all that the omnipotent Creator, whose tender compassion notices a sparrow's fall, may be fitly reverenced by hosts and guests . . . .*

The Trapps ridge south of Mohonk was included in the first purchase by The Mohonk Trust. At Cope's Lookout in 1969 a ceremony was held to commemorate this event by setting a plaque in a large boulder.

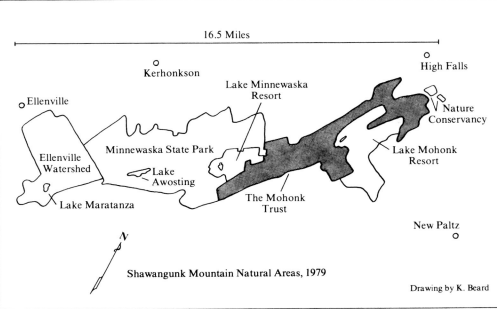

16.5 Miles

Kerhonkson

High Falls

Ellenville

Lake Minnewaska
Resort

Nature
Conservancy

Minnewaska State Park

Lake Mohonk
Resort

Ellenville
Watershed

Lake
Awosting

Lake Maratanza

The Mohonk
Trust

New Paltz

N

Shawangunk Mountain Natural Areas, 1979

Drawing by K. Beard

(Opposite) A local school regularly uses a portion of the Trust's land as an outdoor classroom.

(Top) The Mohonk Trust annually sponsored three-day consultations for international student leaders for ten years.

(Bottom) The major tracts of undeveloped land in the Shawangunk mountains provide a 16½-mile long corridor.

Chapter Seventeen

Toward The Second Century

"Our 100th year is the springboard to our second century."
Mohonk Bulletin, *June 1, 1969*

As Mohonk prepared to celebrate its 100th anniversary, the time was propitious for reflecting upon the wisdom of the past while implementing plans for the future. The stewardship of earlier generations had been augmented in varied forms of service by later family members. Albert and Daniel Smiley had arrived at a simple formula for operating Mohonk: integrity in all dealings, moderation in all things, protection of the land, resistance to fads of the moment in favor of timeless virtues, and a catering to the whole person rather than just to the need for entertainment. It was a formula modern, even daring, in its time. As seen through the pages of this story, it was an ethic severely tested by the whims of society and the reality of wartime and Depression, as well as spiraling inflation and energy crises. Though this formula set Mohonk apart, it became the irresistible draw which beckoned people to come back again and again.

As the June 1, 1969 *Mohonk Bulletin* proclaimed:

> *In years to come there will be more leisure than ever, and more money. Vacationists are going to demand much more than bars and bingo and double rooms with double baths. They will want challenge for the mind and growth for the spirit; they will demand good food and good company, but they will want it in an atmosphere which encourages the use of every sense we possess for the greater good of all; in sum, they will want re-creation rather than merely recreation.*

Commemoration of Mohonk's Centennial in 1969 took a variety of forms and activities. Sunday, June 1 was a festival day. In the late afternoon the Smiley family and guests buried the Mohonk Centennial Time Capsule at the putting green. This sealed receptacle contains a variety of Mohonk artifacts of the 1969 era, and in accordance with the notice on the plaque which was subsequently placed on the rock beside the site, it is to be opened at the end of the next one hundred years, in 2069. The Reverend Ralph E. Davis then commented upon Mohonk, its meaning and its future. Following the time capsule exercises, the Smileys invited all guests and visitors to a reception and refreshments in the Lake Lounge. A buffet supper was provided in the Main Dining Room amidst colorful decorations befitting the occasion. Following after-dinner coffee in the Lake Lounge and a song service, a panel of Smiley family members and friends discussed the highlights of the first century and peered into the possible developments of the second.

On the evening of June 6 there occurred a ceremony in recognition of the 75th anniversary of the first of the series of Conferences on International Arbitration which took place annually from 1895 through 1916. Featured talks included reminiscences by retired journalist Louis P. Lochner, who had attended the 1914 conference; Noel J. Brown, Political Affairs Officer with the United Nations, who delivered remarks on the "Present World Situation;" and comments by Warren F. Kuehl, professor of history at the University of Akron in Ohio, regarding the significance of the conferences.

(Opposite) Participants in the Centennial parade.

(Above) The Centennial time capsule being put to rest; it is to be unearthed at the end of Mohonk's second century.

(Above) The wild mountain laurel is a hardy and profusely blooming shrub on rocky ridges.

(Above right) Excerpts from **The Mohonk Chronicle,** a special Centennial news sheet, issued as part of the one hundredth anniversary program.

Other highlights of the 100th anniversary included the dedication of the Albert K. Smiley memorial rose garden, and an address in the Parlor by the Reverend Ralph W. Sockman with appropriate reminiscences about his years at Mohonk and relationships with the Smiley family. There were also a host of special programs, both entertaining and of a serious nature, during the course of the summer. These were announced in a special newspaper, called The Mohonk Chronicle, which was edited in the spirit of a New Paltz village news sheet of a hundred years earlier.

With the 100th anniversary year completed, a definite sense of renewed interest and kinetic energy could be felt at Mohonk. The transition from the 1960's to the 1970's proved to be a time of great significance in the unfolding story of Mohonk.

(Above left) Looking toward the southeast, Mohonk House and grounds.

(Above) Local town officials and friends of Mohonk officiated at the placement of the time capsule during Centennial ceremonies.

Renaissance: The 1970's

"I think our guests come to Mohonk seeking closeness to nature and tranquility of spirit."

Rachel O. Smiley, 1979

A remarkable resurgence of interest in history and an appreciation for the style and culture out of our past became a strong trend in the 1970's. For once it seemed there was no conflict between old and new. The rediscovery by many Americans of the tessellated pattern of our heritage came alongside evolving life-styles and customs. In such an atmosphere Mohonk was "re-discovered" by many people and marveled at as something unique in American life. Designated in 1973 as a place of architectural and historical significance, the Mountain House is listed on the National Register of Historic Places by the United States Department of the Interior.

"In a sense, Mohonk has no rules, although the general public insists that we do," Daniel Smiley once observed. The "rules," he declared, were like English common law, made up by precedent according to the instinctive ideas and behavior of the guests themselves. From the beginning, the guests brought a certain air of preferred habits and customs dictated by the attitudes of the time. The simplicity and open-mindedness of Mohonk's tradition did not insist on a sharp, blind adherence to custom. Private automobiles, once banned, are now permitted. The no-arrivals-or-departures-on-Sunday policy is now a thing of the past. Similarly, bridge and dancing are today accepted entertainments. The significant point is that the essential Mohonk of substance is adhered to by guests because the Smileys refused to become tied to procedures. It may be considered something short of a societal miracle that the following customs have survived into the second hundred years: jackets and ties at dinner; a daily ten-minute worship service; the Sunday morning non-denominational religious service; the Sunday evening hymn sing; Smiley family-led nature walks, slide shows and lectures; and the absence of a cocktail lounge.

In earlier times guests made longer stays at the Mountain House, and thus were able to learn more, on their own, about the resources that could be enjoyed than is now possible for those who can make only brief visits. Even in the "less organized" years members of the Smiley family and staff provided many opportunites to enjoy group activity, both indoors and out. There were regattas on the lake, bowling tournaments, nature walks, cave exploration, treasure hunts, and a variety of games and contests.

As summer visits shortened and more new people came to the mountain in all seasons, gradually it became clear that some guests enjoyed being a part of groups which were pursuing other interests and hobbies than sports and games. It was not difficult for members of the family and their friends to respond to this need, especially as numerous program areas were compatible with their own individual avocations. A stimulating by-product was the satisfaction of seeing persons who were lonely or were entrapped by dull jobs respond to the pleasures of companionship in common interests.

(Opposite) The golf course provides scenic views and challenging natural terrain.

(Above) The original of this certificate hangs in a Mountain House hallway.

(Above right) Annual Lake Mohonk Tennis Club Tournaments have been played since 1921.

(Right) A Photographers Holiday class receives instruction in close-up picture taking.

The result of this evolution of guests' needs has been the rapidly multiplying list of Mohonk's planned and sponsored holidays and special weekends. (For a full listing the reader may examine the chronology at the end of this volume, but should recognize that individual programs come and go, according to demand, so that in this respect the chronology reflects a trend but is never completely up-to-date). Though some of these events, such as Garden Holiday, organized hikes, and a number of nature programs, started a number of years ago, a marked increase in the variety of such activities has occurred during the 1970's. As this volume is being written toward the end of what may truly be called "the decade of Mohonk organized holidays," a look around the calendar, in a recent year, would list a good number, if not all, of the following: What's in the Winter Woods?; China Week; Pioneer-Sugaring Weekend; The Ides of Mohonk Mystery Program; Runners Rally; Earth Watch Weekend; Tune In To Life; Hikers Holiday; Birding Weekend; Hudson Valley History Holiday; Photographers Holiday; Nature Week; Tennis Week; Music Week; The Art of Stargazing; Garden Holiday; The Holistic Way; and the October Fest of Chamber Music.

The 1970's marked a national resurgence of interest in matters concerning physical health and bodily appearance. Additional sports facilities and programs were designed to augment existing opportunities such as shuffleboard, tennis, horseback riding, golf, hiking, and lawn bowling. The first organized ski tours, complete with equipment rentals and lessons, were inaugurated in 1970. Two new all-weather tennis courts constructed in 1977 became centers of increased activity in line with the national preoccupation with tournament tennis. By 1979 two platform tennis courts were also in use. Following a popular and effective trend, one no longer sees only hikers and walkers upon Mohonk roads and trails, but now runners, joggers, and ski-tourers huffing and puffing their way to fitness.

Because this account was prepared toward the end of the 1970's, and because it is not only a story of an institution but also of the people who have made Mohonk, it is appropriate to discuss personalities currently active in Mohonk affairs. Much has been noted of the work that Dan and Keith Smiley do with Mohonk. Keith remains actively involved with the business, while Dan has turned his attention to The Mohonk Trust, where he serves as administrator. Ben Matteson, as executive vice president, takes responsibility for day-to-day operations, and confronts the labyrinth of state and federal regulations affecting the Mohonk business.

In Chapter Fifteen reference was made to the decision of Gerow Smiley, oldest son of Francis, to take up the practice of veterinary medicine, and leave the partnership. In the spring of 1979, after an absence of some fifteen years, he returned to Mohonk and has taken the position of General Services Manager, with extensive responsibility for the stewardship of the grounds and park areas. He supervises maintenance of roads and trails and also the outdoor recreational facilities.

It was noted in preceding pages that the Smiley wives play an important role in the success of this century-old business. In 1968, in an oral history interview between representatives of the hotel collection of the Olin Library at Cornell University and Dan and Keith Smiley, the question of the role of the Smiley women was raised. Dan Smiley responded with an explanation which underscores the important part they continue to play:

> "In the older generation of Uncle Albert and Grandfather (Daniel Smiley) there usually was one of them who was interested in the garden and had something to say about what seeds were ordered and sometimes flower arrangement, and others who have been involved with entertainment, from playing the organ or playing the choralcelo which was the forerunner of the present organ, to participating in musical programs or

Ski-touring on Eagle Cliff Road. This sport has become one of the most popular winter activities in the 1970's.

(Top) Bird watching is one of the many nature programs which offer evening lectures and regularly sheduled nature walks.

(Bottom) Cave exploration among the many cracks and crevices, an activity of long standing, requires old clothes and tallow candles.

(Right) Mohonk roads and trails offer health-ful exercise to those who run alone as well as to those attracted by Runners Rally weekends.

arranging for our non-denominational Sunday services. My mother (Mabel Craven Smiley) did that for some thirty-five years. She corresponded with the ministers and saw that somebody greeted them when they arrived, and so on. And our wives do a great many different things, including arranging for certain holidays where there's hiking or garden activities or a nature week. And they've all had part in the social activities, being present at teatime, and doing different things to make the guests feel comfortable. . . . They have a very important part in the conduct of the business."

At the time of this writing, Rachel Orcutt Smiley, whose first association with Mohonk is related in Chapter Nine, continues to arrange for the weekly music programs at the Mountain House. She is a frequent participant as one of the artists in the musical evenings and also plays the organ for worship services. She has planned many of the evening entertainments. Through the years, she has added to the homelike feeling through her concern for the well-being of her many friends who come as guests.

With the appointment of Ben Matteson as Executive Vice President in 1969, his wife, Rachel Smiley Matteson, became fully involved in the business. Having been brought up "on the mountain," she was already well acquainted with many guests and staff. During recent years she has planned the interior decoration and supervised the work on flower arrangements.

Marion Bonnell Smiley, with past service in guest service areas, housekeeping, and Gift Shop, presently organizes the Pioneer-Sugaring Weekend program featuring early American crafts. Alice Plumlee Smiley, whose previous experience at Mohonk included musical programs, activities, and interior decorating, now coordinates the annual October Fest of Chamber Music.

Virginia Viney Smiley died in August 1974 after a long illness. Her singing voice and other musical gifts, her writing talents, and her assistance to her husband Dan's work form a significant chapter in Mohonk's story.

Ruth Happel Smiley (Mrs. Keith) has assisted in a number of functions over the years. She is presently devoting her time to consulting about landscaping and the flower gardens, and to photography, including periodic exhibits of her scenes of Mohonk and other natural areas. Also, she assists with photographic and nature programs, and is the coordinator of the annual Garden Holiday.

Bringing a background of library and archival work to Mohonk is Jane Rittenhouse, who married Dan Smiley in 1976. In the light of her prior experience she has very appropriately become Keeper of Mohonk Records and Librarian for the Mohonk library and its special book collections.

As part of the effort to maintain continuity in the Mohonk enterprise, there has recently developed a plan to involve younger members of the family in providing suggestions for the Mohonk business, and in the process becoming familiar with Mohonk's problems and potentialities. These Smiley relatives meet periodically for two or three days of discussion, and include members from as far away as California and Montana.

Two platform-tennis courts were added to the sports facilities in 1979.

MOUNTAIN SIDE

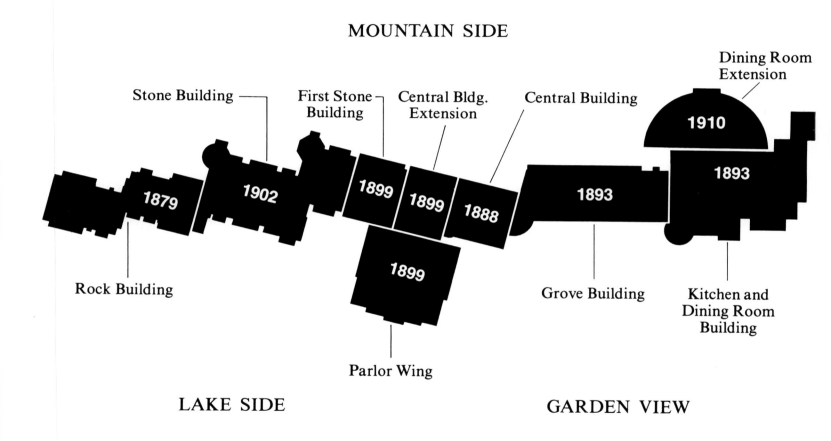

Dining Room
Extension

Stone Building

First Stone
Building

Central Bldg.
Extension

Central Building

1910

1879

1902

1899

1899

1888

1893

1893

Rock Building

1899

Grove Building

Kitchen and
Dining Room
Building

Parlor Wing

LAKE SIDE

GARDEN VIEW

Just as people have been concerned with Mohonk's physical heritage, i.e., the Mountain House, furnishings, and the land, so too were some family members exploring the future disposition of the museum and archival materials at the Mountain House. Haverford and Swarthmore Colleges were recipients of large amounts of research material, and in the 1970's the Smileys effected transfers of the Mountain House business records to Cornell University, and the personal family papers and matters dealing with California to the A.K. Smiley Public Library in Redlands, California.

In the same spirit a Barn Museum was created in the Mohonk stables. The sheer size of this structure gives the effect of many "barns" connected by passageways. In that immense structure (where horses live and regular barn-associated work still proceeds) are housed lithographic fruit and citrus labels; blacksmith implements; over fifty 19th-century antique carriages; old cars; farm implements; and even chamber pots. There are a number of antique items which can be purchased at the museum. An active program of repair, restoration, and the making of saleable items accompanies the museum displays.

The resurgent interest of Americans of the 1970's in their own heritage has touched Mohonk as well. A lengthy article by Ada Louise Huxtable appeared in *The New York Times* on the fascinating features of the Mountain House's architecture. *The New York Times* later did a feature-length story entitled, "Mohonk: Rest, Chat, Rest, Stroll, Rest." Articles appeared in a diverse series of publications that include *Travel Magazine, Americana, Eastern Airlines Magazine, Modern Maturity, New York Magazine,* and the *Chicago Tribune.* It would take a full-time bibliographer to keep updated the list of the stories written about Mohonk by appreciative guests and visitors since its inception in 1869.

(Opposite) Plan of Mohonk Mountain House, showing the chronology of existing sections as they appeared in 1980. Several earlier buildings were replaced (see Chapter 6).

(Top) A popular Mohonk program is known as the Ides of Mohonk Mystery Program. Here Isaac Asimov joins Carol Brener, program leader, in an informal discussion.

(Bottom) Mohonk's Barn Museum uses a part of the old stables.

Chapter Nineteen
Mohonkers And Employees: People Making The Difference

*"This is a family home rather than a hotel and this is what we
... who have spent the most time here feel most strongly."*
                    Thomas G. Ritch, Mohonk guest.

The guests known as "regulars" often refer to themselves as "Mohonkers." One knows that they have arrived at a certain status when they are the object of the remark, "Oh, you know so and so. He's an old Mohonker!" Just when the term "Mohonker" began or how it originated is not certain. It is an affectionate sobriquet for those guests who spend many days on the mountaintop year after year.

Some of the guests, because of their relationship with the Smiley family or because of particular contributions made to Mohonk or to the nation, are known as "Tall Mohonkers." To begin listing these men and women would take a chapter in itself. Many of their portraits may be seen hanging on the walls between the Grove Parlor and the Main Dining Room.

Another group that has consistently filled out the Mohonk experience has been the House physicians. Medical care for Mohonk's guests was rendered from 1870 to 1897 by Dr. S. W. Gerow, who daily (and more often) drove from New Paltz with his horse and buggy to minister to the sick. Dr. Gerow was succeeded in 1897 by Dr. Edward P. Swift, who continued until 1934 as mid-season resident physician, supplemented early and late by one or two other physicians. Since Dr. Swift's time, some physicians have come to Mohonk for a month's stay, some from as far away as California, while others from nearby New Paltz come for shorter intervals.

Another quality that Mohonk has provided since its early inception has been a morning prayer service approximately ten minutes in duration conducted by family members. The Sunday worship services have been presided over for years by a number of clergymen representing a wide variety of denominations.

For thirty years from 1875 to 1905 Dr. Theodore L. Cuyler, nationally known Presbyterian clergyman, speaker, and author, served in what he called the position of "The Mohonk Episcopus." Dr. Cuyler and his wife Anna became close friends of the Smileys and his portrait hangs on the wall of the corridor leading to the Main Dining Room.

Succeeding Dr. Cuyler as resident minister for the summer was Dr. William H. P. Faunce, president of Brown University. For more than twenty years he conducted the church services in the Parlor. From time to time leading clergymen occupy the pulpit of Mohonk; a partial list of distinguished ministers includes Lyman Abbott, Edward Everett Hale, Samuel Eliot, Robert James McCracken, and Theodore Cuyler Speers.

A service provided by Mohonk for the guests might be listed under "recreation for the mind" and is a rich part of Mohonk's history. Musicians, lecturers, and singers have provided entertainment. The lectures have included stirring addresses on world affairs, as well as travelogues and nature programs. Where but at Mohonk could one find a well-dressed dowager examining a boa constrictor at a lecture on herpetology? Where but at Mohonk can guests hear an inspiring lecture

(Opposite) Mohonk flower garden workers of the 1920's, including head gardener on extreme right.

(Above) In the 1920's and earlier the employees' baseball team competed on Saturday afternoons with teams from surrounding towns.

(Above) This 1921 employee band gathered musical talents from many departments and included a driver, a gardener, a waiter, carpenters, and others.

(Above right) A team of young managers was brought together under the leadership of Daniel Smiley (rear, with hat), the general manager, in the early 1900's. A number of the young men later went on to distinguished hotel careers.

(Lower left) Albert Smiley with his long-time friend, Theodore L. Cuyler, who entered into all aspects of life at Mohonk.

(Lower right) William H.P. Faunce and his wife were close friends of three generations of Smileys. Albert Smiley had invited him to attend early Mohonk conferences and he continued for a number of years as "Mohonk pastor" during the midsummer.

on the life of a great newspaper editor and clergyman? Where but at Mohonk might a guest sit on a balmy August evening listening to a Chopin nocturne amidst the burnished wood and Victorian ambience of the Parlor?

"Whatever success has been attained in the management of the estate," Albert Smiley remarked, "has been due largely to the faithful and efficient service given by heads of departments as well as by the great body of our employees . . . ." In the years that followed that statement the business organization chart became progressively more complex. Details of the organization and the people holding important positions cannot all be mentioned. In the early days the position of manager and the attendant responsibilities could with hard work be held by one person. Throughout Mohonk's history the Smileys have enjoyed success for the most part in securing dedicated managerial talent. For example, Albert Leroy was a mainstay of support for Daniel Smiley, just as Daniel Smiley had been for Albert. H.C. Phillips, a pioneer in direct-mail advertising, also managed many of the business arrangements for the Indian and Arbitration Conferences. By the 1960's management technique faced a rapidly changing business climate. Ultimately such positions as executive vice president and resident manager became necessary to continue Mohonk's quality service and to deal with the increasing burden of government laws and regulations.

Certainly the continued service of loyal employees is a key part of the family atmosphere at Mohonk. The chance to come year after year and greet a favorite employee and see familiar faces provides a sense of continuity that is often absent in the rapid personnel turnovers of modern-day business. A person familiar with Mohonk is not surprised to see advancement made from within the staff. In 1899 Albert Smiley made some observations about the close relationships between Mohonk and the employees. It is not only insightful but appropriate for today:

> Civil service is in this house and we believe in it. We take bell boys and advance them, and they are soon regular clerks. Our head cook was night watchman . . . . Our head waiter was trained in here, and we train all our men from the ranks. The steward is one of McCloy's boys, grown up here, and in winter manages a large hotel in Florida, and some of our clerks and other employees are going down with him. Our head farmer has been here twenty years, a very good man, and we always hold on to a good man when we can, and the man who has charge of our mechanical works, was brought up as a bell boy; he trained himself by studying. We recognize men by their merit.

The Activities Staff has played an important role at Mohonk through the years. This picture was taken in the 1970's on the occasion of a reunion of former staff members.

1870

1870's

Evolution of
Mohonk Mountain House

1880's

Epilogue

*"The members of the Smiley family .... have always operated
the property primarily for people who desire to enjoy wholesome
recreation and simple pleasures in beautiful natural surroundings ..."*
From Statement of Principles *of Smiley Brothers Trust*

Today's guests at Mohonk are handed upon arrival a small form which notes: "The traditions of Mohonk Mountain House have altered considerably since 1870 when it was founded. The following information is provided so that you will not be unprepared for the few remaining customs which might, to some, be unexpected." It goes on to delineate and amplify upon some Mohonk requests, highly unusual from the normal course of affairs at a resort hotel. Mohonk has adapted to new situations while maintaining the bedrock of its principles. Indeed the business presently runs under a set of guidelines known as the "Statement of Principles."

The future of Mohonk has been provided for through a mechanism which will allow trustees to guide the operation along the lines established by the Smiley family, should there come a time of no direct involvement by family members. It is likewise unusual to find a commercial institution in business for well over one hundred years still seeking with unflagging effort to serve the whole person.

The story of Mohonk is more than a history recounting dates and facts. Over and over again the guest is touched by the influence of years of tradition, blended with a steadied vigor of purpose. And thus our story becomes a romantic tale, telling of beauty, spiritual refreshment, and human concern.

1900's

Everyone has a favorite spot in the Mountain House. For some it is on the porches, or beneath the large pictures of Southern California in the Grove Parlor. For others it is the quietude of a particular summerhouse or one of the many conversation areas in the main house. For the author it is in the Parlor, somewhere near the quiet ticking of the great grandfather clock, for here amid the rich wood and quiet elegance speak the voices of Mohonk's past. Here also speak the voices of its present—the many speakers, the musical programs, the lectures, and the worship services.
Here, too, is the spirit of Mohonk's future. And it is in this Parlor that one can almost hear Albert Smiley speaking those piquant words at the dedication of the Testimonial Gateway which have served as Mohonk's guide:

> *I trust that many generations of people will pass through that portal and climb the mountain through fine scenery, over well built roadways, and find on the height not only a well ordered hostelry, but more—a home where warmest greetings will be extended and friendships cultivated.*

The Smiley Family

Members who have lived at Mohonk and their immediate forebears.

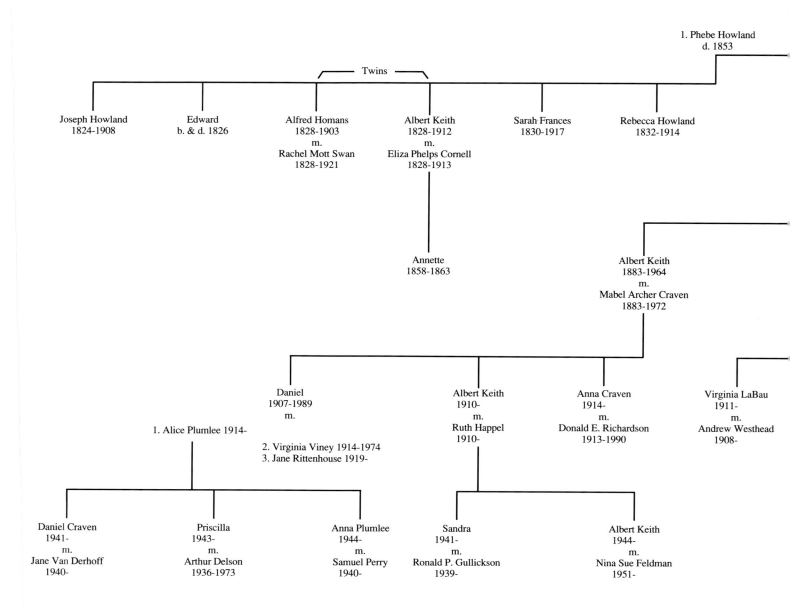

1. Phebe Howland
d. 1853

Twins

Joseph Howland
1824-1908

Edward
b. & d. 1826

Alfred Homans
1828-1903
m.
Rachel Mott Swan
1828-1921

Albert Keith
1828-1912
m.
Eliza Phelps Cornell
1828-1913

Sarah Frances
1830-1917

Rebecca Howland
1832-1914

Annette
1858-1863

Albert Keith
1883-1964
m.
Mabel Archer Craven
1883-1972

Daniel
1907-1989
m.

1. Alice Plumlee 1914-

2. Virginia Viney 1914-1974
3. Jane Rittenhouse 1919-

Albert Keith
1910-
m.
Ruth Happel
1910-

Anna Craven
1914-
m.
Donald E. Richardson
1913-1990

Virginia LaBau
1911-
m.
Andrew Westhead
1908-

Daniel Craven
1941-
m.
Jane Van Derhoff
1940-

Priscilla
1943-
m.
Arthur Delson
1936-1973

Anna Plumlee
1944-
m.
Samuel Perry
1940-

Sandra
1941-
m.
Ronald P. Gullickson
1939-

Albert Keith
1944-
m.
Nina Sue Feldman
1951-

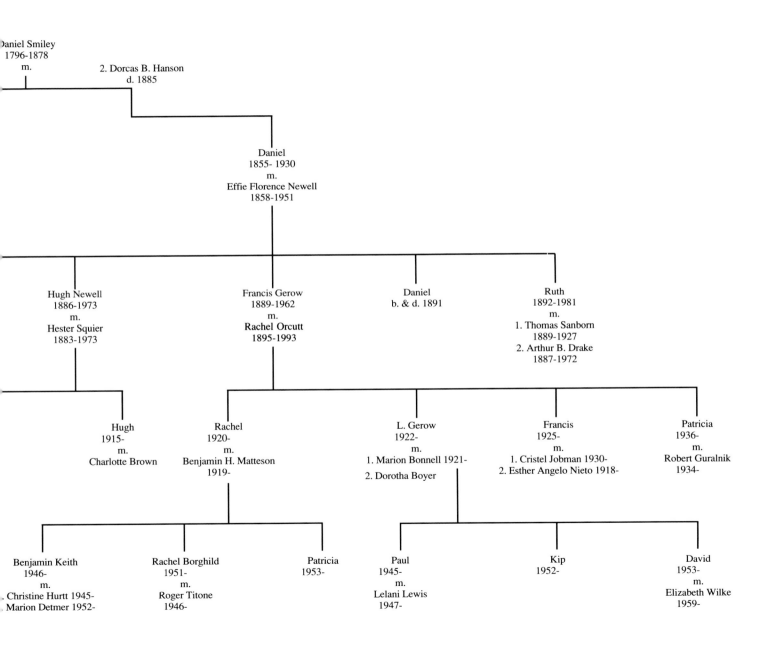

Daniel Smiley
1796-1878
m.

2. Dorcas B. Hanson
d. 1885

Daniel
1855- 1930
m.
Effie Florence Newell
1858-1951

Hugh Newell
1886-1973
m.
Hester Squier
1883-1973

Francis Gerow
1889-1962
m.
Rachel Orcutt
1895-1993

Daniel
b. & d. 1891

Ruth
1892-1981
m.
1. Thomas Sanborn
1889-1927
2. Arthur B. Drake
1887-1972

Hugh
1915-
m.
Charlotte Brown

Rachel
1920-
m.
Benjamin H. Matteson
1919-

L. Gerow
1922-
m.
1. Marion Bonnell 1921-
2. Dorotha Boyer

Francis
1925-
m.
1. Cristel Jobman 1930-
2. Esther Angelo Nieto 1918-

Patricia
1936-
m.
Robert Guralnik
1934-

Benjamin Keith
1946-
m.
. Christine Hurtt 1945-
. Marion Detmer 1952-

Rachel Borghild
1951-
m.
Roger Titone
1946-

Patricia
1953-

Paul
1945-
m.
Lelani Lewis
1947-

Kip
1952-

David
1953-
m.
Elizabeth Wilke
1959-

(Top) The Rondout Valley in earlier times contained numerous small farms and large areas of cleared land. Many seasonal workers for Mohonk were drawn from local farm families.

(Bottom) The Rondout Valley today has fewer active farms than fifty years ago and much larger areas of woods, thus becoming a "rural suburbia" for residents who are employed in nearby towns and cities.

Chronology of Mohonk

1869 Mohonk Lake first visited by
Alfred H. Smiley
Original 300 acres bought by
Albert K. Smiley

1870 The House opened for its first
season June 1st
Wallkill Valley Railroad completed
to New Paltz
Old Stage Road built, being the first
in a series of new carriage roads
constructed between 1870 and 1910

1871 Alfred H. Smiley joined his brother
Newlin's Cave discovered
The first of a series of paths and trails
developed for the use of the guests
(Labyrinth Path marked)

1872 Wooden observation tower at Sky
Top erected

1873 Telegraph office installed

1874 First Dining Room Building built
(It was used as a dining room until
1893, when it was converted to
bedrooms and renamed the
Garden Wing.)

1875 Lake stocked with black bass

1876 Bowling "Saloon" with four alleys
built (now called the Council House)

1879 Albert K. Smiley appointed to
Board of Indian Commissioners by
President Hayes
Alfred H. Smiley opened the Lake
Minnewaska House
Rock Building constructed

1880 Eagle Cliff Tower built
Rock Building in use

1881 Daniel Smiley became manager
First Office Building erected

1882 Post Office established at Mohonk
Second Sky Top observatory in use

1883 First Lake Mohonk Conference of
Friends of the Indian convened
Electric call bell system installed in
165 guest rooms (replaced speaking
tubes in hall)
Livery stable built in present garden
Two lawn tennis "grounds" built, west
of Grove Building

1885 Mountain Rest Boarding House
opened

1887-88 Old Parlor torn down
Central Building built

1888 Bust of Sagonaquado presented by the
Lake Mohonk Conference of Friends
of the Indian
New stables built, stalls for 12 horses

1890 First Mohonk Conference on the
Negro Question.

1891-92 Grove Building erected, first used
in 1893

1893 Present Kitchen and Dining Room
first used
Electric lights installed, machinery in
former ice house
First hydraulic elevator installed
Small Reservoir built and new water
system laid out

1895 Conference on International
Arbitration held its first meeting
in June

1896 Cooperative Weather Station
established at Mohonk

1897 Golf "Grounds" laid out (9 holes)

1898 Garden Road (originally called
Bicycle Road) built
First private bathrooms installed

1899 Long Office and Lake Reading Room
demolished to make way for new
construction
Parlor Building completed

1900 First Illumination of the Mountain for
Fourth of July
Second hydraulic elevator installed

1901-02 Garden Wing torn down

1902 Long distance telephone service
inaugurated
Bugle replaced the old Office
Building bell, to announce meals and
entertainments
Fountain erected in memory of the
Garden Wing
Stone Building first used

1903 Golf Clubhouse built at Mountain
Rest

1904	Indian Conference renamed the Lake Mohonk Conference of Friends of the Indian and Other Dependent Peoples Parlor clock presented to Mr. and Mrs. Albert K. Smiley by members of the 10th Lake Mohonk Conference on International Arbitration Mohonk springhouse dedicated in August
1905	Greenhouse built Athletic field first used
1906	Sundial presented by Mr. and Mrs. James P. Burrell
1907	"Golden Day" Celebration for Mr. and Mrs. A. K. Smiley with groundbreaking for Gateway Second Picnic Lodge opened
1908	Testimonial Gateway dedicated, on October 14th Kleinekill Lake (Duck Pond) constructed Mohonk Hose Company founded
1910	Dining Room circle extension erected New tennis courts built First Putting Contests
1911	Publication of *The Story of Mohonk* written by Frederick E. Partington Main kitchen extension built
1912	Croquet Court laid out *Mohonk Weekly Bulletin* Vol 1, no. 1, May 11, 1912 Albert K. Smiley died at the age of eighty-four Daniel Smiley became proprietor
1913	Eliza P. Smiley died
1915	Choralcelo presented by members of the Conferences, September 25th
1916	Motion pictures first shown on June 5th, on an outdoor screen Automobiles first used at Mohonk: a Ford and two Overlands

1917	Both Arbitration and Indian Conferences discontinued because of wartime conditions Motor trucks first used, Federal trucks with solid tires Radiators in every room, last Franklin stove removed
1918	Mohonk "Country Fair" first held, August 6th, for benefit of French War Relief
1919	Tablet commemorating the Golden Anniversary of the first opening of the House presented to Mr. and Mrs. Daniel Smiley by Mr. and Mrs. James P. Burrell
1920	Fiftieth Anniversary Ceremony June 1st Mohonk School founded Lake stocked with trout Game refuge posted
1921	Cornerstone of Albert K. Smiley Memorial Tower laid August 30th First Lake Mohonk Tennis Club Tournament Accommodations available in winter for the first time, in connection with the Mohonk School
1923	Dedication ceremony of Memorial Tower, August 30th
1926	Sky Top Reservoir finished, for fire protection Mossy Brook Spring water pumped to the House
1930	Death of Daniel Smiley at the age of seventy-four Smiley Brothers became proprietors; Albert K. Smiley and Francis G. Smiley were the first partners
1931	Log Cabin repaired (originally built about 1771)
1932	*The Story of Mohonk* republished, containing Part Two, 1911-1931 First Mohonk Trail Riders Saddle Trip in October (last rides, 1942)

1933	First hiking trip of the Shongum Outing Club, in September
1933-34	Part of Mohonk House first kept open for guests during the winter
1934	Ice skating rink first maintained on the lake
1935	First rock climbing activity on Trapps Cliffs First "Garden Lovers Holiday" (renamed Mohonk Garden Week, June 1941)
1940	Lawn bowling green first used Mohonk's woodland put under management of a full time forester
1943	Last burning of charcoal by open pit method in Trapps.
1948	Shuffleboard court built
1951	Death of Effie F. Smiley
1953	Incorporation of Mohonk land and buildings (Lake Mohonk Corporation organized)
1957	Two new shuffleboard courts constructed near athletic field Buffet suppers inaugurated for occasional evening meals during main season
1958	First alternating current used at Mohonk, supplied by Central Hudson Gas and Electric Corporation First annual Photographers Holiday, in September The Mohonk School ownership transferred to Mr. and Mrs. Edward M. Lafferty. School moved to new location and renamed the Mohonk-Cragsmoor School
1960	Bowling alley at north end of lake rebuilt for meeting hall and renamed the Council House
1961	First Mohonk Nature Week program, in June
1962	Death of Francis Gerow Smiley at the age of seventy-three

1963 The Mohonk Trust founded

1964 Dedication Service of Francis Gerow Smiley Memorial Organ on June 23
Last harvest of natural ice from the lake
Death of Albert K. Smiley at the age of eighty-one
New Smiley Brothers partnership consisting of A. Keith Smiley, Daniel Smiley and Gerow Smiley

1965 Fern and Wildflower Trail established at edge of garden lawn
Granary building moved from deer paddock and renovated for light meal service near tennis courts and bathing beach

1966 First conveyance of Mohonk land to The Mohonk Trust for preservation as open space

1967-68 Two automatic electric elevators installed, replacing former hydraulic known as "Big Elevator" and bellmen's stairs

1969 Dedication of Albert K. Smiley Memorial Rose Garden on July 8
Mohonk's Centennial Year celebrated. Various special events from May to October. Time Capsule buried at the rock in Mohonk putting green. "The Mohonk Chronicle" issued.
Smiley Brothers partnership reorganized as Smiley Brothers, Inc., continuing to lease the land and buildings from Lake Mohonk Corporation.
Benjamin H. Matteson appointed Executive Vice President

1970 First organized ski-touring with equipment rental and lessons provided.
Mohonk receives "Connie Award" for outstanding service in the cause of conservation, preservation, and beautification, from Society of American Travel Writers

1971 First Mohonk Travelers Holiday, in October
N.Y. State fire watch at Sky Top Memorial Tower discontinued. Fire observers had served there in summer since 1921

1972 First Sap to Sugar Weekend, in March, later called Pioneer Weekend
Mohonk Barn Museum first opened, in May
Death of Mabel C. Smiley

1973 Lake Mohonk Mountain House Complex recognized as a place of architectural and historical significance and listed on Natioanl Register of Historic Places by United States Department of the Interior
Merger of Lake Mohonk Corporation into Smiley Brothers, Inc., April 26

1974 First Antiques, Architecture, and History Holiday, in June. Later called Hudson Valley Holiday
Death of Virginia Viney Smiley

1976 First Tune In To Life Program

1977 Two new all-weather tennis courts constructed
New Greenhouse constructed
Riding ring built at site of former ice house

1976-77 The following Mohonk programs were inaugurated:
Mystery Fans Weekend, Earth Watch, The Art of Stargazing, Holistic Way, and the October Fest of Chamber Music

1979 Two platform tennis courts in use
Gerow Smiley joined the organization as General Services Manager
Telephones installed in all guest rooms

1980 Decision by N.Y. State Court of Appeals confirming The Mohonk Trust as a charitable institution
Mohonk Consultations established
Publication of Mohonk: Its People and Spirit, by Larry E. Burgess (1st edition)

1981 The Mohonk Trust name changed to Mohonk Preserve
Grove Building entrance built, with related improvements

1982 Computer installed
Completion of sale of land by Smiley Brothers Inc. to Mohonk Preserve

1983 Fitness Center opened

1984 Archives moved to Oak Cottage

1985 Mohonk Preserve occupied Bonticou Lodge as their headquarters
Bernard L. Gavin became President of Smiley Brothers Inc.

1986 National Historic Landmark designation

1987 Minnewaska State Park enlarged by New York State acquisition of remaining Minnewaska resort property
Installation of new emergency power generator

1988 Donald D. Woodworth became President of Mohonk Mountain House

1989 Death of Daniel Smiley at the age of eighty-two

1990 Albert K. Smiley became President of Smiley Brothers Inc.
Conference House opened

1992 Air conditioning installed in East Dining Room

1993 Death of Rachel Orcutt Smiley at the age of ninety-eight

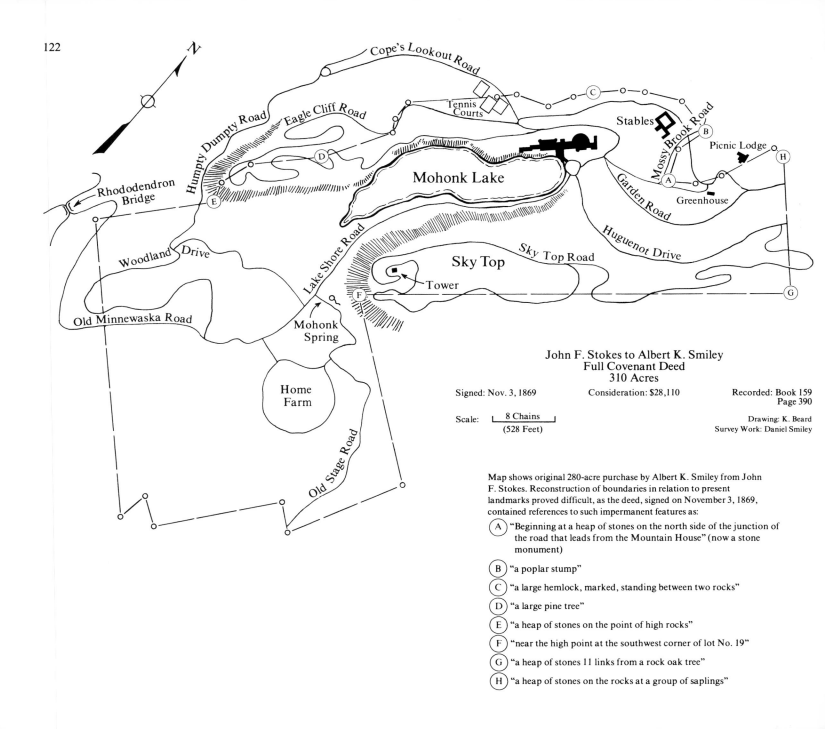

122

N

Cope's Lookout Road

Humpty Dumpty Road

Eagle Cliff Road

Tennis Courts

Stables

Mossy Brook Road

Picnic Lodge

(C)

(B)

(H)

Rhododendron Bridge

(D)

Mohonk Lake

(A)

Garden Road

Greenhouse

(E)

Huguenot Drive

Woodland Drive

Lake Shore Road

Sky Top Road

Sky Top

Tower

(F)

(G)

Old Minnewaska Road

Mohonk Spring

Home Farm

Old Stage Road

John F. Stokes to Albert K. Smiley
Full Covenant Deed
310 Acres

Signed: Nov. 3, 1869   Consideration: $28,110   Recorded: Book 159
Page 390

Scale: 8 Chains
(528 Feet)   Drawing: K. Beard
Survey Work: Daniel Smiley

Map shows original 280-acre purchase by Albert K. Smiley from John
F. Stokes. Reconstruction of boundaries in relation to present
landmarks proved difficult, as the deed, signed on November 3, 1869,
contained references to such impermanent features as:

(A) "Beginning at a heap of stones on the north side of the junction of
the road that leads from the Mountain House" (now a stone
monument)

(B) "a poplar stump"

(C) "a large hemlock, marked, standing between two rocks"

(D) "a large pine tree"

(E) "a heap of stones on the point of high rocks"

(F) "near the high point at the southwest corner of lot No. 19"

(G) "a heap of stones 11 links from a rock oak tree"

(H) "a heap of stones on the rocks at a group of saplings"

Index

Illustrations are indicated by italicized page numbers and footnotes by italicized *n*.